MW01234033

Hiking the Appalachian Trail

By
Chris "Cleanshave" Miller

This book describes the author's experience while hiking the Appalachian Trail and reflects his opinion relating to those experiences. Some names, trail names, and identifying details of individuals mentioned in the book have been changed to protect their privacy. Many of the characters have been combined from a variety people to simplify the overall narrative.

Unauthorized duplication or distribution of this material in any form is strictly prohibited. Violators will be prosecuted to the fullest extent of the law.

No part of this publication may be reproduced, stored in a retrieval system or transmitted in any form or by any means, electronic, mechanical, photocopying, recording or otherwise, without prior written permission from the author/publisher.

The author, publisher, and distributor, of this product assume no responsibility for the misuse of this product, or for any injury, damage and/or financial loss sustained to persons or property as a result of using this report. While every effort has been made to ensure reliability of the information within, the liability, negligence or otherwise, or from any use, misuse, or abuse of the operation of any methods, strategies, instructions or ideas contained in the material herein is the sole responsibility of the reader.

ISBN: 978-1-300-06363-6

Copyright © 2012 Chris Miller - All Rights Reserved

Table of Contents

Introduction

It all happened so fast.

After months of waiting, one moment I'm squeezing pus out of my big toe trying to get my shoes on, hungover from drinking too much the night before, and the next I'm on an Amtrak train bound for Atlanta, Georgia.

The pus is from my attempt at a practice hike.

Less than half the weight of my full pack with brand new hiking shoes and I still only managed to do five miles on a heart friendly loop in a nearby state forest.

And I'm paying for those miles with a painful limp and stained sock.

Rain splatters against the window of the train. Some railroad crossing in the middle of Connecticut, red lights flash, the warning bell and mechanical arms have stopped traffic and I realize that I'm doing it. I'm really going through with this. After all that time waiting, I'm on my way south to Springer Mountain and my Appalachian Trail thru hike.

The knot forms just a little in my stomach and I wonder what exactly have I gotten myself into.

I had never hiked before so I had no idea why exactly people would want to attempt to walk 2,183 miles from some random mountain in Georgia to another random mountain in Maine.

Those two states aren't even close together.

But it's some kind of tradition; some kind of annual pilgrimage undertaken by thousands of people each year. Most of them don't make it all the way, that's the part that caught in my mind. It was a challenge and not everyone was guaranteed success.

That's what I wanted.

A challenge.

First Days

Hotlanta.

Intensity radiated from his piercing blue eyes, and yet William, my host for the night in Atlanta, had a very down to earth feel about him. The relaxed jeans, the Abe Lincoln beard maybe, the fact that he took in strangers and let them crash on his couch?

Whatever it was it took me several blocks before I realized that I had left my backpack, just about everything I owned at this point, in his house on the floor of his living room. Sure, he had given me a key I thought, stopping in mid-stride on the sidewalk on the way to go sight seeing in mid town, but I never tried it in the lock.

I looked back, the older house with sparse furnishings no longer visible, and thought about going back. Back to check the lock, back to check on my bag, to touch it and make sure it was still there, safe. I was sure William had to get back to work, that's why I excused myself after our brief encounter. But maybe that's just what I was supposed to think. He wasn't just being kind when he took out his laptop and showed me a few points of interest within walking distance, Piedmont Park, CNN Center, the Aquarium and Five Points which he explained was the hipster hang out.

He was trying to get me to leave.

"Shut up, you're acting crazy," I said out loud to no one in particular.

Not a cloud in the sky and I had to force myself to keep walking, breathe in, exhale.

He wouldn't steal my pack, would he?

My hike hadn't even technically started yet and already I was suffering from Pack Separation Anxiety. Like when you see homeless people carrying multiple bags at the same time, it is because they don't want to let anything out of their sight.

It is all they have.

Someone right now could be coveting my stuff.

The fact that I had met him online didn't make me feel any better.

I take my shoes off in the park to try and relax, to let my feet breathe. There are newly formed blisters on my feet and under my toes.

They burn and ache.

"What am I getting myself into?" I ask again.

There are two other hikers at the North Springs Marta station.

Their pack weights, almost the first thing I ask about, are 44 lbs and 54 lbs respectively. With food but no water. My base weight is 18 lbs with 10 pounds of food giving me a grand total of 28 lbs without water. A full 16 lbs lighter than either of theirs.

It makes me a little nervous to be so much lighter. I have never hiked before and I'm not sure, maybe I don't know what I'm getting myself into.

Old Duck is older, retired and planning on taking his hike slow.

"Just going to hike until I don't want to hike no more," he says when I ask if he is a thru hiker. Gator, on the other hand, has new shoes and is planning on going all the way.

There was one other hiker, only she wasn't hiking, she was going home.

She had made it as far as Neels Gap, and she was done.

Survivor Dave, well known for being a shuttle driver had dropped her off and was in the middle of picking up another couple. The only reason I hadn't gone with him as a shuttle driver was because he didn't have a hostel, and I felt I needed one more night to make any last minute changes.

OK, maybe that's a lie. Truth is a bed, shower and breakfast were my last tenuous hold on civilization. Kind of like one more night with your favorite teddy bear before your parents take it away and you have to grow up.

Dave himself had previously attempted a thru hike and made it only as far as Fontana Dam before damaging his legs on the steep descent, ending his trip. This was his year though. He was going to pick up at Fontana Dam and continue north to finish his hike.

Our shuttle driver Lee arrives. She thru hiked in 2000, but we're waiting for one more hiker. When he finally arrives his pack is easily twice the size of anyone else's, and he is wearing jeans. A frowned upon hiker faux pas but I'm secretly jealous. At the hostel he is going through his pack trying to get rid of some weight, everything looks like he threw it in the night before and that he has no idea what he actually brought. He doesn't have a trail name and someone dubs him Too Heavy because everyone needs a trail name.

It's tradition...

Hikers back from doing the approach from Amicalola gather around to look at his gear spread out on the back deck, trying to do anything but talk about how bad their day was, except you can see the strain on their faces and in the way they do little things, the way they smoke their cigarettes.

Like they were just in a car accident.

I overhear one on the phone, telling people back home how brutal it was, how they weren't prepared, how there are no leaves on the trees and the sun burns you relentlessly. If he hadn't looked at me right then and saw me listening I'm sure he would have started crying.

Most of us turn in early. It gets dark fast and Old Duck is the first to start snoring. A heavy, loud vibrating sound that shakes the small bunk beds where we sleep. I hear Too Heavy turn in the dark and a click from a backpack clip.

"Ear plugs?" I ask out loud to the deep dark night.

"Yep, just thought I'd be prepared in case it got worse," Too Heavy replies.

Ear plugs, that would have been nice I think staring at the blank space where the ceiling should be. How hard is it to smother an old man with a pillow I wonder?

They do it all the time in the movies.

If you are brave enough, or strong enough you'll probably want to do the approach from Amicalola. While it isn't required for official thru hiker status it is a bit of a tradition.

Listening to the hikers who attempted it the day before you would think that the only reason would be to see the waterfall after which that section is named, the steps going straight up the waterfall and no sun cover were reasons to skip it.

You know, for your physical and mental well being.

It never occurred to me that these were all hikers that failed to easily complete the approach. It sounded brutal and painful, and it had me rethinking my plan to skip it entirely. Painful and challenging? Why wouldn't I do it? Too Heavy hadn't decided yet either, I wasn't real sure he had planned any of the trip. But the weather changed our minds for us, it was foggy, zero visibility. No waterfall, and let's be honest it didn't count as part of the "official" miles.

Why hike it?

The shuttle drops you off in the parking lot below Springer Mountain. The driver points out the trail, "Go that way," he says, "When you see the plaque you are at the top. Turn around and head back to the parking lot and continue north." He continues pointing in the other direction.

This should be easy I think, less than a mile with no pack, come back and get it from the driver and start my trip north. But he pulls everyone's packs out of the van.

"Why is everyone putting on their packs, isn't he going to..."

Nope. He is back in the van ready to leave.

"Good Luck," he says disappearing down the road, fishtailing and cackling maniacally now that he has stranded us here in the fog.

In the middle of nowhere.

Chatahoochee? What is that anyway?

Shit, I'm not leaving my pack here. Strap it on and hike, hike the easiest I have ever hiked, easier than any of those five miles I did before leaving. And this is a climb. Right to the plaque I had seen in all those pictures online.

The First White Blaze.

This is going to be a piece of cake.

I just want to take this opportunity to let everyone back home know how awesome I am.

Take my picture next to this plaque.

See how I'm smiling, it's because I made it. Even after you tried to kill me, I made it here. All by myself, without any of you. And I am going to walk all the way to fucking Maine all by myself.

Even if it kills me.

Because I would rather be dead than go back a failure.

Now might be a good time to explain why I am trying to hike the Appalachian Trail. As I mentioned I had never been hiking before. I did a little bicycle trip down the east coast, from Rhode Island to Florida and being back to work after that killed me. I started drinking more than mortals are allowed if they want to continue living, which is good because I hated my life.

More than appropriate considering the fact that Christmas Eve, and I'm not a big holiday guy, I received the best present ever. Someone tried to kill me. Only they cut the brakes on my car instead of just shooting me in the face.

A rookie mistake.

At 5:30 pm, Christmas Eve, the entire population of the surrounding cities decide that the family needs to go out for Chinese food.

Did I mention that I work in a Chinese food restaurant?

By 6 pm the restaurant is full, each waiter having received between 5 and 7 tables of at least 6 or more people. If you have never waited tables then this may all sound meaningless to you.

It's not a math problem.

Think of everyone you know wanting the same thing at the same time. Then imagine that it is your job to give it to them with a smile.

Never mind that there is a two hour minimum wait for any take out order, the deluge of table orders overwhelms the cook staff and most tables end up waiting at least an hour if not more for the simplest of appetizers.

Chicken wings become like gold for the servers and Pupu platters, a major staple of Chinese dining have a tendency to disappear if gone unwatched by your server as they attempt to wait on the other tables.

Then there are the extra tables placed in the function room to take care of the overflow. A great idea but without extra servers it just becomes a burden on the few of us deemed good enough to handle the extra work.

And when certain servers are unable to handle the massive, immediate influx of tables the elderly Chinese owner wants you to handle their tables as well.

Since they all came in at the same time they all leave at roughly the same time, their tables being immediately filled with more cranky families that have been waiting since six o'clock, having arrived just minutes too late to be seated.

By the time the second round of families has eaten it is now almost 9 pm and the rush is officially over. In four hours you can easily make well over $200 in tips despite that fact that the tips reflected the customers dissatisfaction with the amount of time the food took to be served.

That is $200 for what they perceived as being a bad server. Some tables refused to tip at all, and that hurts because as a server you work hard to make sure that everyone gets their food in the order, sorry, sequence, that they ordered it.

But most people have never worked in a restaurant, or even in customer service.

What made this night even worse was the snow storm.

Blizzard conditions.

Stay off the streets and in your home the news kept telling people.

By the time I walk out of the restaurant, too embarrassed to tell you how much I actually made, the snow was still falling. Everything was quiet and covered in white. I warmed up the car while I cleaned off the snow.

Everything was normal.

Except it was Christmas.

After midnight.

There was no jingle of bells, no sound of reindeer hooves. There was only the sound of snow being compressed underneath my tires and my brake pedal hitting the floor of the car when the light down the road turned red.

At first I thought the car was in a slide on the icy snow packed road. The way it had seemed to lose control when I was leaving the parking lot of the restaurant. I managed to steer the car into the massive snow bank on the side of the road which offered the perfect buffer with which to slow me down.

And I laughed.

I had no brakes.

Seriously? Who does that?

The ride home was a series of controlled crashes into convenient snow banks to slow the car down. At home I gunned the engine to insure that it cleared the snow banks piled in front of the house knowing that I would sell the car for scrap rather than repair the brake lines.

But why would someone want to kill me?

Seriously, me?

I'm the nicest guy you never met.

Well, there is that guy I put in jail a week ago.

He is out now and for some reason the cops told him who called in the complaint.

But he was beating the shit out of his brother, punched him in the face and knocked out most of his teeth while their girlfriend screamed for help.

Cops had to subdue him with a taser.

Then there is the father of a girl. I liked her friend, mostly I was drunk.

They drank.

I ended up cutting my finger on a broken chair when we tried to move her passed out body. I couldn't get it to stop bleeding. My blood was everywhere, she was passed out. With no other bed where else would I make out with her friend?

How was I supposed to know that they were barely old enough to drink?

Or that her roommate would call the police just because of a bunch of blood all over their apartment?

Then there's the car mechanic whose father was found dead...

Well... let's just say the list isn't narrow.

So that was Christmas.

Here on the trail there was so much fog, but somehow it seemed to be a respite from the direct sunlight that I had anticipated. The scorching sun had been the thing that allegedly killed those early thru hikers I had seen at Hikers Hostel.

Maybe killed is too strong of a word.

I didn't need the sun block I had borrowed out of the hiker box.

Didn't need the baseball cap I borrowed from another, older thru hiker ready to give up.

Too Heavy and I made it to Hawk Mountain Shelter.

How we ended up hiking together is that we started at the same time and hiked at the same pace. Sure we passed other hikers, a family that had turned around and given up on the idea of a thru hike. The kids sat down in the middle of the trail and refused to do any more hiking. But it was our first day, and it was only 1 o'clock.

The skies opened up and the rain kept us at the shelter for lunch with a few other hikers. A couple of guys out for the weekend and another hiker hiding in the back. He had done the approach trail and his feet hurt. This was as far as he was making it today.

It was his second day on the trail.

Too Heavy was eager to hike despite the early excitement of the hike having worn off. This was starting to feel like work. But there was no way I was going to back down and not put in the miles to Gooch Shelter like I had said the night before. 15 miles now seemed like a lot more than I could handle.

We had been hiking for a while when we came across another hiker with his gear pulled out of his pack and spread around on the ground. He was holding a small green plastic box with a crank knob and some wires coming out of it. When we got closer he looked up, eyes desperate and pleading.

"Do you have a cell phone?"

Too Heavy looked back at me, I just shook my head, I did but there was no signal.

The guy let out an exasperated breath and returned to cranking the hand generator, trying to trickle charge his cell phone.

"I never should have let the battery die..." he says more to himself than to us.

"Is there anything we can do?" Too Heavy asks.

"I just need to get off this mountain," he whines still cranking away.

We look at each other and shrug. "Good luck."

The trees opened up to a dirt road not too far past him and then the trail took a steady turn upwards for the ascent of Sassafrass Mountain, the first real climb of the trail. I'm taking baby steps trying to keep up with Too Heavy and lean against a tree. Seeing me stop he decides to take a break. I try to let my heart catch up with me.

"Can you believe that guy?" he asks.

"Really, if it is so bad just put up your tent and call it a night," I say.

"Right, do more miles later."

14

Then we both hear it, the sound of a vehicle coming up the road. And through the leafless trees we see the guy pulling his stuff out in the open.

"Looks like he was able to call his friends after all," Too Heavy guesses.

The truck pulls into view and he flags them down. They aren't his friends. Even from up the trail we could hear his desperate voice asking them for help.

"Do you have a cell phone I could borrow?" he begs.

Faintly we hear a "No, sorry," from inside the truck.

"My cell phone is dead, can I just plug it into your cigarette lighter for a couple of minutes so I can call a taxi?"

But it is a mother and daughter in the truck and the answer seems to be the same because they drive off seconds later leaving him there in the middle of the road. We look at each other and start hiking up the mountain.

Another hiker quitting already.

From that point I imagined satellites from outer space watching my baby step progress up each and every climb. One foot in front of another, heel to toe. Shuffling along.

Heel to toe.

"Can't you lift your legs any higher sissy?!" The voice in my head demands.

"No sir, I can't."

Heel to toe.

Do it again.

Again, again, again. And soon it looks like some progress has been made. Sweat pours off of me, my heart races and my mouth is full of thick saliva that threatens to choke me.

Halfway there.

What did I get myself into?

Just off the trail there is an exposed rock big enough to lay on and the pack comes off and I let the coolness of the rock absorb some of my body heat. The wind picks up just a little across the valley moving the fog over us through the still leafless trees.

Fantastic.

My legs were shaking and I still had four miles to go. A sip of water and I realize that the water in my hydration pack is undrinkable.

Don't be like me.

Don't buy a new water bladder and fill it up the first time out on the trail where you will need it.

It will taste like plastic.

And not good plastic. Acid, stomach turning, taste bud burning plastic.

Fill it up at home and dump it out. Fill it up and let it sit for a couple of hours. Dump it out. Do it again and this time run all of the water out of the drinking hose.

Maybe that will help.

Or maybe just don't buy the cheapest hydration bladder you can find at Walmart.

A look at the companion guidebook says that there is a creek a mile before you get to the shelter. The problem with the companion, which has become obvious the first day out, is that it lists a lot of the gaps but not the mountains.

So while I'm out here cursing Hightower Gap and swearing up a storm at Horse Gap I'm actually yelling at the wrong location. It is the mountains in between the gaps that I should be angry with; that and the fat lazy bastard that decided to come out here and make me hike them. Which is me. So just because the elevation between here and there doesn't look too bad doesn't mean that it is at all accurate.

Justus Creek. That's what what I kept repeating to myself over and over trying to motivate myself to keep going. Justus Creek. Water.

Then you hear it off to the right of the trail and your pace picks up trying to find that point where the two cross paths. The trail starts descending and you get a little more excited. So dehydrated. Just a little more, almost there. Then you trip and stumble and you remember that you have all that weight on your back and have to force yourself to slow down.

So thirsty.

And the water is cold and feels amazing when you splash it over your head.

Too Heavy is there already drinking cupfuls he has scooped out of the creek. No water treatment. And it is so tempting... just take a sip to cool off, you'll feel so much better.

But I pull the water filter out of my pack and look for the directions.

That's right, directions.

So here's another little helpful tip for would be thru hikers getting ready for their first day out on the trail: Become familiar with your equipment before you leave home. Don't read the instructions for your water filter while sitting next to a stream when you are dying of thirst.

Too Heavy was chatting up another hiker while I focused on re-hydrating.

"... hiking south. Yeah I just passed by Gooch Shelter, I didn't take a look but it sounded full." The guy was saying. And just then another hiker emerged from a blue blaze trail on the other side of the creek and turned up the trail towards Gooch Shelter.

One mile to go and the shelter was full.

You have to be kidding me.

I shouldered my pack and was off, no blue blazing hiker is going to beat me to a shelter just because they cheated. I wasn't even sure where that path went to or where they had come from, I just knew he wasn't going to beat me to the shelter.

Too Heavy was stuffing spoonfuls from an MRE into his mouth still talking to the other hiker when I lost sight of him. I was sweating in no time and my feet hated me. But I hated that other hiker more and kept going.

I want to sleep in the shelter. I don't want to sleep in my home made tent the first night out. Honestly I was embarrassed of the thing and hoped now that I wouldn't have to use it at all. The tent was part of my bright idea to make some of my own equipment and go light. It was a tube tent made from two 55 gallon contractor garbage bags taped together in the middle.

I had set the thing up in the woods near my house before leaving but it had been rolled up since and tied in place on my pack. I wasn't going to use it tonight.

I passed the other hiker after a half mile with barely enough breath to say hello and lost him far behind. The strange thing was that I wasn't already at the shelter. I kept expecting to see it, climb a little more up this hill and it will be there, but it never was.

"I had to have gone over a mile by now," I said out loud. "I did more than a mile already." I repeated over and over again looking at my feet shuffling down the trail. In a daze and aching in my knees, shoulders and back. My leg muscles lacked the energy to keep hiking.

Where was this fucking shelter?!

Through the trees I caught a glimpse, and there were a lot of people standing around, cooking dinner, chatting. My heart sank a little but I had made it this far so I ambled up and took a look.

"Any room?" I asked unable to put together a more complex question.

"Shelters mostly empty," someone piped up, "everyone is tenting."

And sure enough, no sooner had the words come out of her mouth than I noticed the multitude of tents, hammocks and even a tarp set up and spaced out through the area. I peeled off my shoes and sweat soaked socks, spread out my EZ Lite mattress and made sure to save a space for Too Heavy.

I didn't move until after he arrived. Even then it was only to get water. I'm probably the only person that filtered from the spring but what the hell, it was practice with the water filter and this time I didn't even have to read the instructions.

The one thing I wish we did have instructions for was hanging the bear bag. It had seemed so simple in the descriptions I had read online before I left, but here there was a bear cable set up that was already full with peoples food bags.

What was the etiquette? Was I allowed to attach my bag to the same clip as someone else? What if someone stole my bag, or mistakenly took it? Making matters worse, most of the bags were identical brands and colors.

So we decided to use my bear rope; Too Heavy hadn't brought one of his own.

First we couldn't get the rope up over the bear cable to hang it. Then it looped itself around the cable and wouldn't come down, Too Heavy apologizing profusely for losing my rope and caribiner.

Frustrated I gave it a solid yank and the metal clip came flying back at us with an amazing amount of speed and force.

"Let's try it with a small food bag on it. Maybe that will be easier."

So we throw the bag, only it hits someone else's bags and manages to knock open the clip and send their bag plummeting to the ground with a loud thud. We look at each other and look around to be sure no one saw and start laughing. The clip isn't broken and since we have to bring the cable down to reattach their food we may as well attach our own bags to the same clip.

There are at least 20 people at the shelter and it starts to fill up as it gets dark. The mattress isn't as comfortable as I thought, having tested it on the carpeted floor at home wasn't really the ideal comparison. Too Heavy starts snoring and mice are scurrying around. I lay there awake for a while worried about my new pack hanging from the shelter wall.

I'm so tired but I don't really sleep.

I drift in and out of consciousness more than anything else. It is going to take some time to get used to sleeping outdoors. It was much easier sleeping in the haunted bedroom.

Before I left for this little adventure I didn't really have my own apartment. After I got back from the bike trip my plan was to make enough money off of my websites to allow me to travel full time. Only that didn't happen as fast as I imagined and I ended up bouncing around a lot.

When I heard a friend had a room she wasn't using I jumped at the chance.

It started with a simple question.

"If I pay half your rent can I sleep in your unused bedroom?"

After a few seconds pause, reflecting on the fact that she is short on rent money a week into the new month she asked, "You know its haunted, right?"

That's why she didn't sleep in her own bedroom, because its haunted. She has a ghost in her apartment that sometimes leaves the front door wide open and plays tricks in the bathroom. Make up gets moved, toilet seats get left open and she falls into the cold water half asleep in the middle of the night.

She keeps the bedroom door closed and refuses to to heat the room. It's mostly used for clothing storage and changing.

"The cats aren't allowed in there either," she says.

"There's really no room for you to bring in a lot of stuff..." she adds, hesitating, not wanting to kill the deal. She wants, no, more likely needs the money.

But I don't need a lot of space I assure her. Despite pulling down a management job in a restaurant most of my possessions are in storage or in my backpack. It's not easy but avoiding rent and utilities has allowed me to put away more money in a short amount of time than I had previously thought possible.

And I wanted to hike the Appalachian Trail.

With it being winter in New England, three blizzards in the last month alone, I was in no position to be sleeping outside. Forced to sell my car recently I had few places to go.

A haunted, unheated bedroom was just what I was looking for to save money.

The queen size mattress had fitted sheets, a flower printed quilt in orange and blue on a background of white that worked visually, and several unused pillows. The ceiling was slanted almost to the point of coming into contact with the bed but what the hell did I care, I wasn't outside or in a homeless shelter.

Besides, in most homeless shelters you aren't supposed to drink. And drink I do.

Some point in the middle of the first night there my bladder wakes me from the stupor of being passed out in the cold room, my skin alerting me to the fact that it is only 30 degrees, indoors.

Having slept in my jeans and socks I stumbled towards the bathroom, through the hallway and past the kitchen table where my host sat writing a letter to one of her recently released prisoner friends. There is a 12 year old girl standing next to her that I don't recognize but I say hello to be polite.

Having relieved myself I immediately return to bed, yet in the cold room I am unable to fall back asleep. The little girl seemed out of place somehow. Now that I think about it she shouldn't have been there, there are no little girls that should be in the apartment. There are no neighbors that would have let their kids come over at four in the morning to watch my host write and color pictures to be sent to incarcerated individuals down in Florida.

And that thought wakes me up.

I get out of bed and walk back into the kitchen where she is still working at the kitchen table coloring pictures. Only this time she is all by herself.

I hesitate before asking, knowing how stupid this is going to sound.

"When I just came out here was there a little girl standing next to you?"

I am an idiot.

The look in her eye is clear that I am gravely mistaken. She looks around at the obviously empty apartment, holds up a crayon and shrugs as if to say, "This is it, just me."

She is stoned and half the bottle of wine is missing, but she would probably know if anyone else had been hanging out. I retreat into the haunted bedroom, roll under the quilt trying to shake the cold. The little girl is on my mind.

She was so clear and obvious. Like a "real" person.

So that's how I dealt with it.

I had a roommate that may or may not have been a ghost and had to set down some guidelines.

"I'm cool with you, if you have any problems with me let me know, we'll work it out," I said to the cold bedroom air.

Once that was done I slept, peacefully in that room despite the low 30's temperature.

But the shelters were something completely different.

So many people.

At sunrise I hadn't felt like I wasn't able to get much rest. By the time I had made my protein shake Too Heavy was gone, too anxious to wait any longer. But the protein shakes were my secret weapon, and my major source of calories on this trip. I figured early on that I would get sick of most types of food, especially being "no cook", which only meant that I hadn't packed a stove and didn't plan on eating any hot meals.

The trail was going to beat the shit out of my muscles and consume a lot of calories, so what better way to repair the damage and replace those calories than with whey protein meant for bodybuilders?

I tried a few kinds before I left and found the Walmart Vanilla brand to be appetizing enough that I could stomach it for long periods of time and cheap enough that I could afford to live off of it for several months. When two scoops of protein mix equaled as many calories as a candy bar but weighed much less I was sold.

Then I ran a spreadsheet, boredom and a computer do that type of thing to me, and noticed that the cost per calorie was significantly higher than some of the other foods I was planning on packing. 0.0016845 dollars per calorie higher than a Snickers to be exact.

Not even a penny but with a 5,000 calorie a day requirement that's a difference of almost $8 a day. I needed the muscle building action of the protein but I had to find a way to stretch the calories out.

It's a good thing the vanilla whey protein doesn't taste great in water. The answer? Add milk, powdered milk. I had hoped to find a cheap source of powdered whole milk but even after learning about Nido, found in the Spanish section of some supermarkets, I was never able to try any. For most of the trip I used a mix of non fat dry milk which was cheap enough when bought in bulk that it brought the price down of the protein drink.

The only drawback was that I had to buy equal parts of each, and carry a couple pounds of powder at a time.

But dinners were great, milkshake for breakfast, and another for lunch.

I know it's a catch phrase from something...

Of course if I wanted to save money I would eat only peanut butter to get those 5,000 calories. That would cost me a grand total of $3 per day.

But I wasn't going to eat peanut butter all day, everyday.

No sooner do I leave the shelter than I pass yet another victim of the trail. He was an older hiker and slept at Gooch last night. His hips hurt and he decided, after failing to push any distance today, that he was calling it quits at Woody Gap. Which was just up the trail and the first place you can easily get a ride out. That's what I had heard. I did know from the companion that there was a post office nearby and Too Heavy was going to try to hitchhike to it and send some of his pack weight home.

I still wasn't sure how I felt about trying to hitchhike.

Except that by the time I arrived at Woody Gap Too Heavy was ready to go, he had waited for me before starting. Only no one was pulling over. There were a good amount of people around, it looked like a decently busy spot, plenty of people out cycling in their spandex and expensive bikes.

They just didn't want a couple of dirty hikers in their car. Dirty bikes OK, those can go on the racks and they can shake off their shoes and change into something cleaner before even getting into the car.

Too Heavy wasn't giving up. He was chatting up everyone that came near us, "How are you? Yeah, I'm hiking the Appalachian Trail and trying to get a couple of miles down the road to the post office in Suches... Have a nice day then."

Over and over. It's not that he wasn't friendly, Too Heavy was one of the most genuinely friendly people I have met, picture a car salesman that didn't want to sell you a car and just wanted to make sure your life was awesome.

Like that.

Except for... well, he is totally out of his mind.

He does really well at hiding it but I think most people suspect that something else lies under that friendly inviting exterior. Part of it might be that he is from Maine. I have never met anyone from Maine before and I kind of picture it being like the Texas of Canada. They do everything big except for the fact that they're in the sticks. Out in the middle of nowhere, like a third world country residing within the borders of America.

That's just how I picture it.

When people hear he is from Maine they have to make the joke that, "Hey, you're hiking home." And then they laugh, like it's the first time anyone has said it, and he laughs like it's the first time he has heard it. I just roll my eyes and think about stabbing boring people.

But persistence pays off. Too Heavy manages to persuade a Georgia Appalachian Trail Club guy into giving us a ride down the mountain while he waits in vain for some kind of supervisor of a race taking place on the Appalachian Trail.

Whatever. It's a pickup truck and we ride in the back. Windy as hell and for no reason makes us laugh like idiots the whole way down to the post office where Too Heavy pulls apart his pack and tries to decide what to get rid of. The trail club guy stays, "Reminds me of hiking," he says, "All those times out there maintaining the trails."

"Right here in Suches, I had been working the trail and wouldn't you know it, caught in a storm like you wouldn't believe. Trees blowing down around me, everything I own is soaking wet and muddy. I manage to make my way back down the trail and into town. There's this little laundromat not too far from here and without anything else to wear I looked around to make sure no one was there, stripped almost naked and dried my clothes."

He laughs at the memory.

"Hid in the storage closet in my skivvies until the rest of the clothes were done."

He looks off to the mountain visible behind us and is silent for a few moments. I immediately like him a hell of a lot more.

Too Heavy managed to send home 20 lbs and 9 oz, I'm not sure what he sent, cold weather gear and MRE's mostly but his pack is a ton lighter. We work our way through a hundred or so bikers that showed up at the last minute, just as we were leaving, and back to the trail where the sun cuts through leafless trees and cooks you slowly.

Trillium, fiddle heads and random tufts of grass are starting to show and the hope is that spring will be here soon. Oh joy!

That is sarcasm.

What I do care about is the bear that lives near Woods Hole Shelter, where we're spending the night. It is a full half mile off the trail and at first I think I'm lost. Maybe took the wrong trail. Where the hell is this place and why is it so far away?

I hiked enough already for today, don't you know that?

Frustrated but glad to be in the shelter except everyone is talking about the shelter register.

"There is a bear here!"

We knew it would happen, eventually, that's why we were supposed to all bring bear ropes even though this shelter, like most in Georgia, are equipped with bear cables. Maybe we didn't expect it to happen our second night out but it was going to happen.

Turns out the bear doesn't care about the bear cable. It likes to slap the shit out of them with it's massive paws. And like that food bag the first night at Gooch Shelter the clasp will open from the strain and drop a bag, which is quickly scooped up and taken into the forest for digestion.

Fucking bears.

Why are you so smart?

But I hang my food anyway, like everyone else.

What are you going to do?

The shelter fills up fast and the tenting areas get harder and harder to come by, a couple of guys decide they are going to tent on the last available flat spot, directly beneath the bear cables and everyone's suspended food.

I think it's a great idea, my food will be safe as long as the bear can get to these guys first.

There is a lot of green here and I don't mean in the trees. Most people seem pretty unsure about what they are doing and the conversations all center around gear and food. Stoves mostly.

Almond, his trail name, is a no cook hiker like me so he doesn't have a stove or any input on the different makes and models, no preference for butane or alcohol.

He got the trail name Almond his first day out. He was carrying several pounds each of almonds and raisins. His research before hitting the trail had indicated to him that if he ate a pita smeared with peanut butter and packed with almonds and raisins for dinner every night it would take care of the majority of his calorie and protein needs.

Only he doesn't really like raisins or almonds and it takes him almost two hours to eat the whole thing. He has to build up courage between bites just to get the thing finished.

Another hiker from Texas keeps his diet a little simpler. He pours whiskey from a plastic bag into his cup and sips while we all listen to another hiker explain that he is out here hiking after failing to set the Bass Pro Fishing world on fire with his abilities.

"Those guys are ruthless," he says, "it's a cut throat sport."

Everyone is eager to embrace trail culture and part of that is having a trail name. I think it's silly. A secret name you use only out here that sets you apart from all those people back home.

Oh you're so special.

So I have a hard time not rolling my eyes when the hiker from Texas asks everyone for some trail name ideas.

You know, these people he just met, just now for the first time in his life.

"How about Whiskey Bag?" I chime in when he doesn't seem to like anything else.

It's a no on that one.

He ends up liking the name Tomahawk, which fits because he carries, yep, you guessed it, a tomahawk. It's original, creative trail names like that inspired me to make up my own before I left. That way someone wouldn't point at my orange Osprey pack like an idiot and and say, "You're trail name is Traffic Cone, cause your pack is orange!"

Naming myself Cleanshave, because I'm not growing a trail beard like most of the other guys, is easier than having to strangle someone in their sleep for making up a stupid trail name.

So the guy getting drunk has an ax. Nobody thinks it's weird.

I'm finished with dinner early, a Snickers and a granola bar don't take that long to eat, so I decide it's about time to try my first privy.

The privy at Woods Hole Shelter is on a hill. A hill that catches the wind. Which I suppose is a good thing for the aerobic breakdown of everyone's poop, but which feels slightly strange when when you sit on the seat and it feels like you have a fan pointed up your ass.

The real adventure begins when you wipe and try to drop the paper in the hole.

It comes right back up at you.

By the time I finish dodging flying toilet paper and get back to the shelter everyone is getting ready for bed, Tomahawk slides his ax into his sleeping bag, "To protect us from bears," he says.

When he realizes that everyone near him is sleeping head out he turns his sleeping bag around to be facing the same way.

"You're my family now," he says to the married couple next to him. Even in the dark I can see them exchange worried glances at each other. I'm guessing they'll be the first ones up and out on the trail in the morning.

During breakfast people are talking about a 3 mile nero into Neels Gap. It is only our third day out and already everyone wants to slow down and sleep in a hostel.

A nero if you don't already know is hiker slang for a low mileage day, like a 'zero' means hiking no miles, a 'nero' means hiking nearly zero miles.

And Neels Gap is an important landmark. Besides the fact that it is the location of the Mountain Crossings outfitter and Walasi-Yi hostel it is also the location by which 30% of all north bound thru hikers call it quits.

All I can think about is cold soda.

Between here and there though is Blood Mountain. The highest point on the trail in Georgia. Some people are so worried about the climb that they are taking the blue blazed Freeman Trail around the mountain instead of taking the official trail up and over the summit.

So damn tempting.

After all my talk back home of this just being a walk it is turning out to be much harder than I had originally thought. My legs hurt all the time and my shorts have actually cut through the skin on my waist. The waist band is being rubbed against my skin by the waist straps on the backpack, there is blood.

Sweating in the heat of the cloudless day I keep telling myself, just a little farther and you can have a sip of water before we start this climb. Then I push the branches aside and climb over a rock and the Blood Mountain Shelter is in front of me.

I made the climb without even realizing it.

Dropping my pack in front of the privy sign I promised myself never to listen to pansy ass hikers talking about things up the trail that they had never seen or experienced before. Blood Mountain was too easy to climb, but I'm glad I didn't plan on staying at this shelter. Besides smelling like mildew the story goes that there are a couple of bear cubs in the area that are good at sneaking in the window to steal food.

Then it's all downhill to Neels Gap.

Once I find my way back to the trail after losing it going over the rocky edge of the mountain that is.

Mountain Crossings is busy. Even from the trail coming down I can hear the car doors being slammed and that sound of people moving around. It is a vague feeling of civilization that leaks through the trees and permeates the side of the mountain.

I'm excited.

Even more so after having a cold Coke and meeting Pix again.

From what I could tell Pix is everything I would want in a girl if I was able to form those kind of relationships. Thankfully she hiked on ahead leaving Too Heavy and myself to enjoy our soda.

There is this game called The Cube that I had played before I left. The idea is simple enough, a few images are thrown out and you draw or describe what you see. It's an exercise in determining how you see your life, or perhaps what you want out of life, and Pix was part of that.

Or someone like her.

Maybe there were a million girls out here with the same mindset, maybe, but I doubted it.

Like I said, thankfully she hiked on. The last thing I needed was complicating my hike with a stupid crush. I was still out of my mind with city scrambled brains.

Too Heavy hiked without his shirt and by the time we get to Tesnatee Gap he is noticeably redder. His hiking pace slows way down and he has to stop for water and shade, the only part of his skin that isn't burnt is the part protected by his shoulder straps.

Turns out Pix had stopped for water as well and she wouldn't mind a little hiking company. So against my better judgment we hiked out together. That's how it starts, people clumping together, all hiking at roughly the same pace, with personalities that don't mesh, all showing up at the same watering holes, the same shelters for the night.

Some people do low mileage everyday, some people get up early, some people stop at a shelter just after noon to call it a day. And you just end up seeing a lot of the same people. Pix, Neon Mud and Padawan had become people Too Heavy and I were happy to see at each stop. We didn't know much about each other, all that mattered was that we were determined to make it to Katahdin.

But you still have to rely on yourself. Like being responsible for your own gear.

There I was on the top of Tray Mountain, wind howling, storm front moving in, and the shelter was full. I wasn't looking forward to it but my homemade tube tent was the only option.

A few other hikers looked on with concern while I strung it up between the two trees behind the shelter.

"Are you sure you're going to sleep in that thing?"

"It'll be all right, I tested it out at home," I said not wanting to mention that I had never slept in it nor did I try it in the rain, but hey, I'm here, let's do it.

It was a lot tighter than I remembered since I also hadn't tried it out with either the sleeping pad or the sleeping bag, but I would make it work. Really, how much would it have to do? Just keep me dry and out of the wind.

Then the storm got worse and refused to let up the whole night. With every movement of my body the slight incline I was on pushed my sleeping pad off to the side, up and around the inside of the tube tents wall until I was sleeping on the bare ground with only the thin wall of the trash bag between us.

Then, in the middle of the night I had to go to the bathroom. It was so tight inside and it was so wet outside that I quickly gave up any futile attempts and resigned myself to holding it.

Besides that it held up remarkably well. The foot of my sleeping bag was a little wet from getting exposed during the night but that could have easily been fixed by leaving the bottom on that trash bag and having more of a sealed tube than an open one.

Finally, just at sunrise the weather broke and I was able to get out of the tent and go to the bathroom.

Peeing never felt so good.

Tribes and Trail Legs

Crammed into the last van out of Hiawasse, there are more hikers than I had anticipated. All heading for Muskrat Creek Shelter just across the Georgia/North Carolina border.

The cramped van full of recently laundered hikers drops us off at Dicks Creek Gap where it is a straight up climb through shaded green tunnels of rhododendron covering the trail and creating atmosphere not unlike hiking in a refrigerator.

I can see my breath and the cool wind feels good on my skin as I climb.

Then there is the border sign.

Georgia/North Carolina.

No small deal, for many people this will be the last big landmark in their hike before calling it quits or maybe section hiking the rest of the trail.

Too Heavy sits up on a rock waiting for Pix, Padawan, Neon Mud and I to show up. We had all spent the night in Hiawassee in the same hotel room and we were fast becoming friends. Despite still being severely sunburned and dehydrated it's obvious that Too Heavy is going to make it to the end.

I know this now, early on the trail because you can tell, not in the superficial way that most people judge other hikers, but by the way he knows himself. Too Heavy has to make it, and on some uncertain deadline that I have not been able to ascertain. Maybe he is yet still unaware of what this whole hike means for him.

I'm pretty sure no one knows why they are really hiking. Sure they have a few pat answers that roll off their tongue when people ask, "I've always wanted to do it", "I want to get back in shape", or the weakest of them all, "I wanted the challenge."

I can't help but to think that growing up in Maine helped him prepare for this. I'm just a fat kid from the sprawl who grew up dreaming about living in the woods with Che Guevara.

Maine may as well be a colder version of Mexico to me.

So, being inexperienced cold Ramen sounded like a good idea.

As I mentioned I am No Cook, I don't carry a stove and I don't heat water. Not even by the fire at the end of the day.

But Ramen Noodles could be put in a water bottle and allowed to soften while I hiked. Throw in the flavor packet and it was just like eating cold soup. Right?

Wrong.

It turns out that you have to heat the water to dissolve the flavor pack. Otherwise it ends up as congealed chicken flavored chunks and a slimy yellow film that coats the inside of your water bottle. I found this out at lunch after leaving Hiawassee.

Even after repeated rinsing you can not eliminate the chicken flavoring from the bottle. So until the next resupply I was stuck with chicken flavored water with every sip.

Cold and overcast.

The combination of fog and cool weather makes the hiking infinitely pleasant. If it wasn't for the blood soaking through my sock I would have enjoyed it more. My ankle is bleeding from the low socks I used the first couple of days. The constant movement of the top edge of the sock being pressed against the back of my ankle by the sneaker wore through my skin.

The limp is more noticeable because my right foot is also a mass of blisters.

Coming up to a ridge line you can hear the wind howl in the trees and stir the leaves around your feet before you reach the top. The wind like the ocean, waves crashing on the shore of the treetops. Then, suddenly you are inside a tempest of wind, swirling around you cold and damp.

The wind is powerful beyond words and I want to stand there forever in it's cool embrace.

Less than a mile later it is too hot hiking with the sweatshirt on, pack it and start hiking just as it starts raining, making you cold all over again. Stopping for a rain jacket is out of the question. After every stop it takes a while for the blistered foot and the open wound on the ankle to get used to moving again. Those first steps are a painful incentive to quit hiking. They'll hurt until you can pound the damage into some kind of numbness.

Get past your own physical limitations.

The weather promises a cold, wet night and Wayah Shelter is all I can think about.

A hiker appears somewhere behind me and I know I have to hurry, limp faster, to make sure I get a spot in the shelter. Except the hiker is a machine, a huge German farm boy named Freyr also intent on making it to the shelter.

We're both too late.

The other hikers are listening to a weather forecast and the storm sounds like the worst one so far. Forget the garbage bag tent, I'll sleep right here on the floor. Neon Mud is right next to me and Too Heavy, as always seems to be the case, is already squeezed in the shelter somehow, the last person to get a spot and already snoring.

Freyr puts his tarp across the opening to give us some cover and it is raining already.

I try to eat a frozen Snickers by the fire to get warm where a younger hiker is telling me that he has been hiking with an old man he met on the trail.

"We're doing low mile days," he says throwing another log on the fire, "I'd like to do bigger miles, but I don't want to leave the old guy alone."

He's lying of course. Though he looks physically fit, he looks too clean, his gear is too new. This isn't what he thought it was going to be, I can tell by the way he looks into the fire, even without saying anything, that he is starting to think about the end.

Maybe a week or more and he'll be gone.

I give up trying to warm myself by the fire and retire to my sleeping bag and reflective bivvy cover. Padawan had arrived later than anyone else and has nowhere to sleep. The rain is coming down hard and he sits on the window sill of the shelter, thinking about what to do? Waiting for a break so he can set up his tent? I'm not sure.

I tell him to squeeze in somewhere on the floor if he wants.

Inside the sleeping bag I'm wearing everything I own. Full thermal underwear, shirt, shorts, socks, sweatshirt, hat and gloves and wrapped in the emergency heat reflective bivvy. The rain slams hard against Freyrs tarp stretched across the side of the shelter and occasionally my face is sprayed by rain.

At least the torrential downfall hitting the roof drowns out the noise of everyone snoring.

The occasional thunder and lightning flash or splash of rain in my face wakes me up. Each time I can see Padawan still sitting there refusing to move from his perch. Soaking wet in his rain gear.

I sleep better than I have on the entire trail so far.

I wake up refreshed. Heel hurts like a bitch, it is cold as hell outside and my sleeping bag is damp, but otherwise...

Padawan is no where to be seen. Took off as soon as it stopped raining someone says as I'm squeezing more pus out of my big toe.

"Strange how he just sat there all night, never sleeping." someone else says.

I limp 11 miles through the river that is the trail before calling it quits.

The bleeding has stopped in my ankle, now it is just an open wound smeared with triple antibiotic ointment. The blisters on my feet are so bad that after I stop I can't rest with my feet flat on the ground, and because of the ankle I can't really keep them propped up.

I hang my sleeping bag out to dry a little, knowing that I'm done for the day. Knowing that everyone I want to hike with is going to get ahead of me. But I'm not thinking about distance, elevation or miles. Despite the pain and possibly losing everyone

I enjoy hiking with I am in the best mood I can remember in a long time.

A group of Canadian hikers comes in and dives into their food bags. Everyone is starving all the time. If you ever listen in to hiker conversations at shelters it usually revolves around food. About the hunger, Hiker Hunger.

Meanwhile I eat a Snickers and I'm good.

The way Wesser Bald Shelter was designed, on a hill and with spaced apart floor boards, the wind is funneled up into the shelter. Cold air blows through the floor of the shelter which is probably great during the warmer summer months, but now when it is in the 20's or below it makes sleeping hard.

Even through my sleeping pad, the bivvy and the sleeping bag I can feel the wind stealing what little warmth I manage to create.

But I had a little secret. It was called gtum-mo, the Tibetan method for creating heat within one's own body to resist the extreme cold temperatures in the Himalayas. Technically there are three types of gtum-mo, but at this point I was only interested in the one that provides physical warmth.

I had read about it one night, half drunk so that I thought I got the gist of the idea, but still had to strip down the details. I practiced it alone several times before leaving, sleeping with the bedroom window open.

The full initiation into gtum-mo takes three years, three months and three days.

I'd had a handful of nights practice, never knowing whether or not to trust in the whole process. To make it worse there were a few restrictions when using gtum-mo, don't use it indoors or near other people. I didn't think the shelter really could be considered indoors, it was a standard three sided shelter, less if you didn't count the floor. But the other hikers sleeping in the shelter could be a problem. The restrictions were probably more of a guideline for preventing bad energy than anything else I tried to convince myself.

That and I never really followed the directions to the letter.

Still, I didn't have much of a choice, I was freezing.

And probably out of my mind that I would trust in an ancient meditative practice to save my life rather than having been better prepared.

Don't let the doubt creep in, it's too cold and there is no other choice.

Exhale completely.

Relax, arms at your side, hands resting comfortably on your hips.

Imagine the color red.

Imagine the red glow inside your body several inches below your belly button. The rest of my body is an empty vessel. Picture the glow, there inside my body and breathe. Exhale through pursed lips, as if you are blowing a glowing ember of last nights fire into a new flame. Imagine that breath is fanning the fire of a new flame inside you. There is a spark and a glimmer of a flame with it's yellow edges lighting up the inside of your hollow body.

Inhale slowly and exhale the same way again, visualizing the breath building the flame like a bellows in a forge. Breathe and allow the flame to grow inside you, illuminating and warming your inside, and allow your blood to pick up that warmth and carry it into your extremities.

Keep it up until the flame reaches a level that fills your whole body with an internal warmth.

Only I was comfortably asleep long before I reached that point.

I woke up shaking from the cold just before dawn and had to go through the whole thing again but I was quickly back asleep.

The third time I woke up it was light enough that I could start hiking, besides which I couldn't feel my toes and thought that maybe I should get some blood flowing to them sometime soon.

The NOC, pronounced "knock", could be heard before I had finished coming down the trail. Voices over loud speakers filtered through the trees, unintelligible but with an enthusiasm that said sporting event.

Multi colored kayaks, cars, people...

... a diner!

I was so damn excited I probably would have killed everyone if they had told me they ran out of food. Food! Bacon, two eggs, short stack of pancakes, and at the table near the entrance, just finishing their breakfast was the rest of the crew, Pix, Neon Mud, Too Heavy, and even Padawan who had hiked to Rufus Morgan Shelter after not sleeping a wink at Wayah Bald Shelter during the rainstorm.

Was it sad that I had identified with a group of people this quick?

At home I would never have given two thoughts about being this happy to see anyone. I didn't even know these people.

They were finishing up, I had just got there. They were planning on spending most of the day here they said. Neon Mud lost a bet that I wouldn't show up and owes Too Heavy a beer. Despite the overwhelming desire for food I simply cannot finish it all, so much for the hiker hunger kicking in.

I sat next to the river drying my sleeping bag out, munching on Chili Cheese Frito's and enjoying the sun.

Why the hell am I so happy?

I have to double up on the band aids to try and keep the blood off of my new wool toe socks. Another thru hiker has suggested them to prevent the blisters I get in between my toes. I don't want them soaked with blood right away.

The hike out of the NOC is straight up.

At one point on the trail you can look down and see the NOC about a mile or two below you, down by the river, and you think to yourself, I just hiked from there, it's an amazing feeling.

Accomplishment and feedback, maybe it's that simple.

Sassafras Gap Shelter is full of hikers getting baked. They have been here all day smoking and tending a small fire but never really collecting firewood. The newest person to arrive collects a little, then smokes a little.

They are talking about their hiking experiences as if they are all Veterans of a war, seen it all been through the shit, man, and lived to tell about it.

"No one ever said they wanted to hike the Appalachian Trail faster," Rooster is saying to Too Heavy when he starts talking about making big miles.

Neon Mud rolls his eyes.

Rooster is hiking the trail with his girlfriend. They have matching sleeping bags that zip together, and besides the obvious depth of his budget this is a major drawback to his making friends.

Also he is a total douchebag.

Anyone who relates a trail related story has to wait and listen while he tells of a much better experience he had that is similar, and yet better.

"It's too bad that everyone is hiking the trail wrong."

I ignore him when he is trying to bear bag his food.

I ignore him when he realizes that most of us have hung our food from the mouse hangs inside the shelter.

"If everyone else isn't going to bear hang their food then why should I!"

It's an accusation more than anything related to the problems he had getting his food up into a tree.

"If everyone wants to take a chance of a bear attack then it is not MY fault when it happens!"

Thank god he went over to reassure his girlfriend that he would protect her, otherwise we might have thought he was frustrated at not being able to hang a bear bag or worse, scared of bears.

Pix comes marching down the trail to the shelter and Too Heavy slams down his hand of cards. If she had waited just 15 minutes, he would have won the beer bet about when she would arrive. Secretly I'm so happy to see her that I wonder if something is wrong with me.

"Did you just say 'happy'?" I ask inside my own head.

Pretty soon we're all in bed. Our various mattresses and sleeping bag combos stuffed into the shelter, a bunch of people tenting and hammocking outside.

The full moon rises above the horizon and the special quality about this shelter is the windows on the top half. I watch the moon rise in the quiet night thinking about how content I am, not just because Pix chose to sleep next to me in the shelter, but overall.

The Appalachian Trail is like a summer camp for adults.

Too Heavy starts his heavy, loud snoring and the hiker on the top shelf wakes everyone up around him as he shuffles through his backpack. He pulls out a long sleeve shirt and ties it in a big knot around his head, the bulk of it over his ears.

I lay awake, not because of the snoring but because of her, lying next to me. Every time she rolls over, in whatever direction, she ends up an inch closer to me.

An inch at a time.

Closer and closer.

I'm the first one awake and packed.

Neon Mud swears that he read on the internet that you can get pizza delivery at Fontana Dam Shelter. Maybe I read something like that, I can't remember, it's just not in the notes I added to my guidebook.

He swears it's true.

On his word we all pledge 22 miles for the day.

Our longest day yet.

"I'll see you when you pass me," Padawan says hitting the trail first.

The rest of the stoners are going to do 10 miles to Brown Fork and call it a day.

Good riddance.

There is no name in the guidebook for the monstrous hill that makes me baby step up it's entire face. One by one, deep breathing, lean against a tree, here and there, I slowly made it to the top.

I hate hiking.

Why am I still doing this?

Eventually you see Fontana Dam through the trees. Then it is a lot of down hills and circling.

Across a road and parking lot. A little over a mile to go and there is a group of hikers who have spent the day in town and are heading for the shelter.

"I swear to god you are not going to get there before me," I say under my breath.

I push myself to climb faster, keep up a good pace. On the downhills I am actually running.

Just to stay ahead.

Then the trail is next to a paved road and for some reason this pisses me off.

This could have been easier.

The group of hikers I had run ahead of arrives at the shelter just minutes after I do.

"Wow, that didn't even seem like a mile," I hear them say.

I want to stab them, put a knife through each one of their cheery hearts. Baseball bat across their stupid heads.

Why do you have to be so happy?

That was the longest mile ever.

Then again their hike for the day was stepping out of the shuttle and crossing the parking lot.

I grab a few spots on the hard to reach top bunk of the shelter. Hard to reach if you have no more energy or muscle coordination in your legs. I'm still hesitant to leave my pack with everything I own, just laying there on the flat plywood bed.

If it was just hikers it'd probably be no problem.

"LoMo," he says waving from his sleeping bag, "you want to buy a Lipton Side?"

Turns out LoMo isn't a hiker. He is a local that has been living in the Fontana Dam Shelter for the last few weeks, aka the Fontana Hilton. He sells Lipton Meals to hikers to pay for his beer runs.

This is his third year here and he usually stays for a couple of months.

Sell Lipton Sides, buy beer.

"Hot Springs is "wet", will always be wet." LoMo assures us and I'm starting to feel like I could use a drink after having to listen to some of the other hikers do nothing but complain.

Complain about the water, the trail markings, the pointless ups and downs the trail takes us over, better known as PUD's.

"They're not PUD's," a voice says from the dark corner of the lower bunk, "They're NUD's, necessary ups and downs. If it wasn't for the climbs we'd have every asshole in the world out here, may as well be hiking in a mall."

The clean looking group of tired hikers all look at each other, another hiker nut job.

Everything hurts and I'm just too tired.

Time for my first zero.

I get ready to say goodbye to everyone, but Pix and Neon Mud decide to zero as well. Too Heavy is anxious to be done, like he expects to finish the hike to Maine in the next few days. Padawan decides to keep hiking at the last minute and says goodbye.

So what do I do on my zero day?

Walk.

Walk down to the dam for a look. Only the visitors center is closed and there are no people around. The American flag is high on the pole, flapping in the wind, the hollow aluminum sound of the pole ringing across the landscape. Cars, empty in the parking lot. No sign of people, movement, of anything.

It's like a Stephen King novel, or the apocalypse.

It feels like there is no one else in the whole world, just me and the wind.

It feels like home.

Not like any of the places where I have lived, something else, a home that is more real than anything I have ever experienced. Part of my brain wonders why that doesn't seem the least bit disturbing while the rest of my brain is far too comfortable to worry about it.

Hours later I have to pull myself away, force myself back to the Fontana Hilton before it gets dark. There the talk once again centers around pizza delivery.

When I mention that I was able to get cell service the phones come out, things get Googled.

"There is a pizza place not too far away but they won't deliver," someone finally says.

Then the lady who said she was zeroing, same as she said yesterday when we got here, mentions that she has a car. Only she'll need some gas money to go pick up the pizzas.

"How much?" the desperate hikers want to know.

"$20 for gas ought to cover it." It seems like an insanely high amount to drive 10 minutes to get a pizza and come right back, only everyone wants pizza.

"If we all split the cost of gas money it'd be about the same as tipping a delivery driver," the hiker most determined to get pizza explains to everyone.

And with that he starts taking orders.

Neon Mud is already gleefully imagining telling Too Heavy that he missed out on pizza.

Luckily the pizza run happened when it did because the Hilton started to fill up with hikers, each seemingly louder than the next.

"Well it WAS a really relaxing day," Neon Mud says nodding towards the new arrivals.

I wander off to charge my phone in one of the power outlets in the bathroom and Pix follows. There's no power in the woman's room so I plug her phone in with mine and we play tic tac toe outside on a board made from sticks she has arranged on the ground.

"Before I started hiking," she says, "I had a friend who had hiked. He said that every group of hikers goes through three stages. First it's gear talk, then personal stuff where everyone shares everything about themselves, then it becomes random talk to amuse each other and fill the time."

"We never really talk about gear do we?"

"No," she says, "and that's what I like about hiking with you guys, we skipped the first two and went straight to the random, amusing stuff to fill the time."

No personal questions seems to be our unwritten rule. I wonder why that is? Every other group of hikers is talking about loved ones back home, troubles with their job or their marriage, but us, we talk about how many more miles for the day, where the water is, resupply. Our talk all centers on the trail and getting things done. Even the lack of gear talk is an understanding that you have what you have and you have to make it work. There is no gear envy or elitism.

We are here to hike.

That's when I realized that for any of us not to make it to Katahdin would take an act of God.

Smokey Mountains

At 6am it is raining so hard that I don't think it will stop all day.

The thought keeps running through my head, "Maybe taking a zero was the wrong thing to do."

I roll over and try to sleep a little longer when some guy with a thick southern drawl leans his head into the shelter and starts shouting. At first no one can understand him and tired hikers turn in their sleeping bags wondering who the hell this guy is.

"Shutting off the water in two hours. It'll be off all day," he is saying a little more clearly this time.

Yesterday someone had decided that it would be a good idea to pull the sink out of the wall in the mens room. Maybe they were sitting on it or hiding drugs up in the ceiling, I don't know. Now they had a repair crew in to fix it and they were eyeballing all of us as lazy no good vandals.

I brush my teeth in the remaining sink and use the toilet for the last time in what will be at least a week. Only it feels funny going to the bathroom. When I get up the toilet bowl is filled with blood. Blood that wasn't there when I sat down.

"Well, fuck."

This could be bad. It's not like it's a little blood, like you just spit from a bloody lip or something. This was thick blood that didn't appear to be watered down from what was in the toilet bowl.

Except I wasn't bleeding now. I stood there for a solid minute looking at it, wondering what to do, before flushing the toilet.

"I'll deal with it later."

I grabbed my pack from the Hilton and reminded everyone that it was going to rain all day, maybe they should take a zero. I wanted to give them every incentive to stay, to get ahead of the noisy group of hikers.

"Are you OK?" Pix asks as I hoist my backpack.

"Yeah, I just want to get out there in the rain and get some miles in," I say. "See you up the trail."

Outside the rain is a heavy downpour. It is the first time on the hike that the rain has lasted more than a few minutes and I'm glad that the waterproofing of my gear will finally be put to the test.

Across Fontana Dam and up the road access to the Smokey Mountains. Once you are off the road the trail seems to climb straight up and despite the cold rain I was starting to get steamy under the collar. It's tempting to pull the jacket off but if it's cold at this elevation what will it be like when I reach the top?

Then it's as if I hiked above the rain and am walking in the clouds. Squirrels and turkeys are spooked from the trail as I approach and the views where the trees give way are breathtaking. The clouds are settled between the various mountains on the horizon, they surround me on every side, and it only takes a shift of the wind to be lost inside another one.

I take a lunch break at Russell Field Shelter and Pix comes up all excited at having seen her first bear. She hadn't even realized what it was until she was right on top of it, then they both got startled and the bear ran off.

Neon Mud shows up as she is telling the story and is disappointed, he had let Pix hike on ahead, that was supposed to be his bear.

My mind isn't really on bears or lunch, or even talking. I'm thinking about bleeding.

"I filtered way too much water, you guys want any?"

"Sure," Pix says pointing to her backpack while munching on some crackers.

Her clear 20oz bottle is strapped to the outside, and removing the lid I pour in the rest of the filtered water. Only the water bubbles.

Water mixing with water shouldn't bubble.

"That's my stove fuel!" Pix shrieks.

Oh shit!

I stop pouring immediately. There's nothing else I can do. We pour out a little on a clear spot on the ground and see if it will light. The flame seems weak and yellow, but it burns.

Out here there's not really much else we can do.

Turkeys gobbling in the mist. Hiking higher, it's like you're in the clouds unable to see more than 50 feet at a time, then you're above the clouds and everything is clear.

Turkeys follow you or run ahead of you on the trail.

Hiking seems to take forever after I tried to pop a blister on the bottom or left heel the day before. Put a safety pin through the flame of a lighter to sterilize it and then squeeze out the pus and clear liquid. Hiking on it hurts. A lot.

And then the woods changed. Pine trees alter the look and feel of our surroundings, everywhere it's like a brand-new trail.

The decent nights sleep just before Clingman's Dome was only interrupted occasionally by the loss of feeling in my toes. By morning I was ready to get the blood moving and packed in less than two minutes. Pix, who had been up eating a hot breakfast long before I rolled out of bed, was ready to go as well.

The rain starts up as soon as we hit the trail. Cold, wet and foggy. What look like awesome views are obscured in the fog and lost on us blanketed in a world of white.

The Dome itself is an awesome view, or so the signs say. The ramp to the top is barely visible when we arrive and long gone after we have stayed a few minutes. And yet it is all still quite mesmerizing. The howl of the cold wind, being soaking wet when Neon Mud arrives, we are all in such high spirits you would have thought we'd won the lottery.

And hiking down is so easy and carefree, there is cold Mountain Dew sodas on the side of the trail, trail magic that has

Neon Mud glowing from ear to ear. And in the parking lot all our worries about hitchhiking disappear when we have an entire family excited to meet real "thru hikers" surround us almost immediately.

The Burbank family offers us beer and cheese. Their grandfather, whom they had brought up the mountain to walk a portion of the trail, is 82 years old. His name is Dick and it was on his bucket list. His name brings no end of amusement to his grandson who laughs every time his grandmother says something to him.

"You want some more of this Dick?"

"You eat all of that Dick."

"Taken out of context it could be the soundtrack for a porn," the grandson is explaining between giggles on the drive down the mountain for resupply.

"He's a real Steve Martin," his father says, "or maybe Richard Pryor."

Resupply is easy, tourists take our picture like we are just another street performance here for their enjoyment. Lunch is at the Smokey Mountain Brewery. Burgers all around and beers, except I order a Cosmopolitan.

"Nothing says manly like a cosmo," I say.

"Yep, a nice pink drink says tough," Neon Mud jokes.

In between stuffed mouthfuls of food we joke about the amenities, running water, air conditioning, power outlets to charge cell phones and cameras.

"You mean you can pee AND poop in there?" Neon Mud says about the toilets in mock disbelief.

"I was wondering why I couldn't find the mulch or a handful of leaves," Pix says.

We eat, we drink, and we laugh all by ourselves, stuck in the corner farthest away from any other paying customers.

Getting out of town takes a little longer but not much. A large pickup truck pulls up driven by a lady in her mid 60's wearing an oxygen mask.

"Hop in the back, ain't enough room for any of you up front."

I figured it was an excuse, for her own safety, but a quick look and she really doesn't have room with all the oxygen tanks she is carrying.

We hop in the back and the laughing seems contagious. Everything feels so easy and perfect.

"I'm headin to Cherokee to gamble," the lady says when we try to thank her. "My sons are cops down in Gatlinburg. They hate that I smoke, gamble and pick up thru hikers."

She eyes us for a minute like she is going to burst out laughing, then puts the truck in gear, "Headin to Cherokee to gamble. Good Luck."

And then she is gone, out of our lives as quickly as she drove in.

The night in Icewater Spring Shelter is cold and exceptionally windy.

Laying in my sleeping bag on the top bunk of the shelter I realize how life's priorities change slightly while out here. At home if you asked me what I was concerned about I might say something about my job or making a rent payment or something else equally silly. Out here my concern centered on beef jerky. I had just purchased way too much in Gatlinburg and with the wind I was worried about my food bag being blown down and eaten by a bear.

Eaten before I could enjoy it.

I would fight a bear for that jerky.

Several times throughout the night, usually after a particularly strong gust of wind, I'd find myself half out of my sleeping bag, ready to go out in the dark cold rain to save my bag of beef jerky. The only thing that stopped me was that the shelter was crowded due to the weather and there wasn't any room to move around without waking everyone up.

A hiker had even strung his hammock from a couple of the ceiling beams to be inside out of the storm.

As soon as a few hikers had stirred in the morning I was up and out for my food bag. The sight of it still hanging made my heart soar. Beef jerky for breakfast!

A rough looking older guy is tending to the fire. I notice a tattooed tear drop under his eye while trying to apply some Neosporin to my raw ankles.

"You should soak your feet in really dark tea the next time you're in town. It'll toughen them up," he says, savoring what looks like a found, half smoked cigarette.

"A cigarette and hot coffee, the perfect hiker breakfast."

I get the impression that it isn't the perfect breakfast by choice and offer some jerky. Then it's a couple Ibuprofen and I'm back on the trail.

Ridge runners pass us a few times during the day and by the time we hit Tri Corner Shelter they are on the lookout for a missing hiker.

"Well not so much missing hiker as abandoned equipment."

"What? Someone just decided to leave all their gear here and go home?" We asked.

"Sure, happens a lot. Usually it isn't everything, but they get sick of carrying all that weight and just leave stuff behind. Then we have to pack it back out." The ridge runner explains.

And by the time we get to the next shelter we can see why, families have made it to the closest shelter to civilization and are doing nothing but complaining and arguing with each other.

"It's your fault I hurt my leg!"

Another kid takes his brother's iPod and won't give it back until he cooks dinner. Others are arguing about who is going to do dishes, an older guy is already snoring and the crowd is giving his sleeping form evil stares.

And for all that it turns out to be one of the quieter shelters so far. Everyone had been so tired that they all fell promptly asleep. Only someone dared to snore. So a weekend hiker had to complain very loudly that this was their worst camping experience ever, they had to do this early in the morning so as to wake up the rest of the hikers in the shelter.

I make a protein shake for breakfast while the hiker continues to rant and notice that the raw red heel of my left foot is starting to fill with pus. My right big toe has finally stopped oozing pus and is now only bleeding. Day 17, just a little over two weeks out and I have finally stopped oozing pus from one place for it to start from another.

Between that and losing blood every time I went to the bathroom you'd think this would be an awful experience.

Instead I couldn't imagine being anywhere else.

Crawl to Damascus

The hostel is right on the trail as it rolls through the center of Hot Springs, NC.

Neon Mud swears he read that the place was haunted but decides to stay there anyway. Despite the beds being in high demand the three of us manage to each get a spot, Neon Mud and I in one room, Pix in another with someone else.

My first priority in town, after eating of course, is to get my foot fixed. Only there isn't much beyond Dollar General for medical resupply. And it turns out that both Padawan and Too Heavy had zero'd here, and would again since we were staying. So after some hydrogen peroxide foaming into my heel, and I do mean 'into', imagine a white hot foaming drill bit going right into your heel bone.

That must mean it's working, right?

Slap on some new bandages and it was time to eat again. And drink beer. Normally I don't drink beer. It doesn't do much for me, taste or otherwise, but, what else am I going to do? Lay around in the haunted bed and breakfast while everyone else goes out and has fun?

So after we took turns shaving each others heads out back with a brand new set of clippers from the dollar store we drank. And bullshitted. Mostly about doing more miles and missing stuff versus slowing down and taking longer.

I realize that this conversation, these same conversations have probably been repeated almost verbatim by every thru hiker, every year, that has made it to Hot Springs and plans on finishing at Kathadin. The beer almost guarantees that their opinions will get voiced.

270 miles of hiking and everyone is talking like they are seasoned veterans of the trail.

Then one of the hostel workers comes in for a few drinks with the hikers. When it becomes apparent that he is striking out with Pix he turns bitter, starts talking bad about the hostel, the owners and hikers in general.

"Hikers don't recycle. You guys come in looking for a place to sleep then leave and disrupt the whole cycle of things." He slurs a little after only a handful of beers. "I hate hikers. I hate this place." He adds hanging his head.

The group of us walk him back to the hostel to sober him up. I crawl into bed, sliding my feet under the blankets when it happens. A small catch, my toenail being caught on the rough surface of the blanket followed by searing pain.

I don't even have to look to know what had happened.

The blanket had pulled my toenail back off of my big toe and over half of it had broken off. Now the raw toe that had been bleeding for weeks was exposed and hurt every time it touched the blanket. At least it wasn't bleeding.

In the middle of the night I'm awakened by the sound of someone talking, and at first I think it's hikers rudely awake too early having a conversation. Then I realize that it is only one voice, and it isn't in English. Someone is talking in their sleep I think and roll over.

In the morning Neon Mud is convinced that I was up all night speaking in tongues.

It's always hard to leave a town. The food, the beds, the showers. And the fact that I left a sizable chunk of toenail in this one didn't make the climb any easier.

The wind is rocking trees and snapping branches. Besides watching the trail I have to keep an eye out for dead falls above that could come crashing down at any minute. A tree to the left of the trail groans and falls to the ground and I'm wondering how much further this damn shelter could be?

Shouldn't I be there already?

Aren't I always asking that question?

Something about the wind and raging storm calms me down. I'm pretty sure that's the only reason the younger, much faster Almonds had refused to move on ahead of me, there is safety in numbers. The more the limbs snapped, the louder the wind howled, the slower my hiking pace. I became absorbed into everything that was going on around me, the sights and sounds, the smell of the earth.

And then sign for the shelter prompted the younger hiker to sprint ahead to see if there was any space. Too Heavy and Padawan had found the last spots in the shelter but squeezed together to fit me in, the other hiker had moved over the hill to a hollow out of the wind to pitch his hammock.

The lightning becomes constant, there is no thunder, only flashes of light and silence except for the powerful wind. And for the longest time there is no rain. I sleep better than I have so far on the entire hike. Something about the storm is comforting.

Late at night hail pounds the steel roof of the shelter which turns into a torrential downfall. Looking up into the dark I realize that though I can't see it, my food bag is directly above my head.

If a bear comes in now I'll be so embarrassed.

The idea is that if anyone tells you they hiked the entire Appalachian Trail without falling once then they are lying. When I left I was determined to be that guy that everyone would think was lying, after all it's walking, how hard could it be to remain standing on your own two feet?

The problem isn't so much as walking, it's what you do while you are walking. Some people listen to music or books on tape, some people sing or daydream. What I tend to do is get lost in my own thoughts, even when my brain clearly screams out, "Don't step on that rock! It will roll and isn't good footing."

You'd think a very clear warning like that would need an immediate response. It should have been a warning sign, instead my body kept walking while a different part of my brain went, "What? What rock?"

By that time I had already stepped my right foot onto it, and for the briefest second I thought, "You were wrong." Then the rock rolled off the trail, down the hill, forcing me into the splits, smashing my left knee down on yet another rock before I am unceremoniously rolled off the trail by the momentum of my backpack.

Ten feet off the trail my brain has one more parting thought, "You're an idiot."

How bad did I smash my knee? It's bloody and I can't bend it. Fuck. Feel around the joint, nothing seems out of place, let's give it a second I think and lay back somewhat uncomfortably.

Just breathe.

Too Heavy comes up the trail, a look of concern on his face.

"You okay?"

"I'll live," I say. "I'll catch up with you later."

"You sure? You want a hand up or something?"

"Nope." After some hesitation he finally leaves. I unbuckle my pack and painfully roll out of it and crawl back up to the trail. A little stiff but it doesn't seem broken. The blood is an issue except that it's only a few more miles to the shelter where I was going for lunch.

And my first aid kit is not exactly on the top of my pack.

By the time I get to the shelter a couple of hikers about to leave gasp.

"Are you all right?" they ask sounding alarmed. I look down at the cut on my knee and notice for the first time that the blood has covered my calf and soaked into the tops of my sock.

"It's just a flesh wound."

34 Degrees.

Wake up and you can't feel your nose or your toes.

Condensation billows above you with every exhale, curled up in your sleeping bag, too cold to get up, too early to try you tell yourself. Only this is the same time you get up everyday.

Just after sunrise.

Even though everyone else is awake and getting ready to go you squirm a little deeper in the bag looking for that elusive warmth. It doesn't work.

Force yourself to move.

Pack your bag and hike up out of the gap as intermittent hail falls through the cold fog that hugs the ground and trees. It isn't wet and the rain jacket stays in the pack being pelted by hail.

It seems like the only sound in the whole world, the static created by hail and everything it touches. No one else seems to be around, driven to Greasy Gap Hostel by the weather, the trail is mine alone.

Half a mile later you start to feel your toes again.

Descending in elevation it grows warmer and soon you're stripping off what clothes you can. Passing slack packers going in the opposite direction, they point out Roan Mountain covered in ice, like an evil witch's mountain castle.

Ice Queen.

"How's Roan?" I ask.

"Beautiful," they say, "a winter wonderland."

"Couldn't have asked for anything more on this trip," the other one chimes in, "All of the seasons in one hike, just miraculous." she says looking back at the mountain they had just crossed over.

Her eyes turn a little harder as she turns back to me.

"It's supposed to get below freezing tonight in town," she warns

6,275 feet of elevation gain means it will be very much colder at the top.

How cold is cold I start wondering hiking on, left alone with my thoughts and the view of the mountain looming before me.

I'm tempted to test out my cold weather gear, not that I have much, and the highest and coldest shelter on the AT would be the place to do that. Really, what's the worst case scenario?

I stay awake all night doing jumping jacks to keep my body temperature up and stay alive?

I laugh so loud at that image that I have to look around and make sure nobody saw the crazy hiker laughing by himself in the middle of the trail.

I had never been one to like the cold. In fact I had started late on the Appalachian Trail because I had wanted to miss any snow or cold nights. When I'd read that people lost the trail due to snowfall by starting in March, or worse February, I decided to start in April.

And still I was worried about being cold.

How cold is cold?

That was the question which found myself on Easton's Beach in Newport, Rhode Island on New Years Day.

Every year there is this thing called the Polar Bear Plunge. New Years morning people line up at the beach and run down into the ice cold ocean wearing nothing more than a pair of shorts.

It sounded idiotic, except for the fact that they were doing it to raise money for A Wish Come True Foundation. That and it was an excuse to go swimming in the ocean in the dead of winter.

Something I wouldn't do unless there was a real reason.

Hundreds of people lined the beach, in costumes and in groups, some still partying from the night before. Then at noon the bell rang and we all surged into the cold ocean water.

At first it was no big deal. I was determined to go out farther than anyone else in the crowd and soon people who had been ahead of me were already running back having gone in only to their knees. Then the crowd grew thinner as fewer of us pushed on to water above our waists.

I dove into the water and started swimming out, away from the others, determined to go farther.

Then, when I thought I was out the farthest I stopped swimming. Treading water I watched all the people screaming and laughing, running back to the beach and towels and blankets held by loved ones and friends.

I didn't feel cold. I felt alive.

Sure my chest was a little tight, it was hard to breathe in too deeply, so I figured it was time to head back to the beach. After a few strokes it was possible to walk, the water only just above my stomach.

That's when I noticed my toes, the extreme pain that seemed to be piercing through a numbness that I hadn't noticed. Like my toes had been put in a fire, and it was spreading. Up my toes into my foot, into my heal and up my ankles.

At first it was funny, then with the water resistance and the fact that the beach was still far away, it became something elsc.

As the feeling started to creep up my legs I wondered if I would be able to keep walking or if I would lose control. If my legs would stop accepting instructions from my brain and dump me head first into the water.

That would be bad.

"That isn't going to happen," I said to myself, determined.

A surge of warmth rolled through my legs, forcing the pain back down to my toes where it had started. Everything else was numb, everything except my determination to make it to the beach. Each lift of the leg, every new step forward had to be the whole focus if I was to make it back.

Then I started laughing.

Freezing in the cold north Atlantic ocean waters seemed so far removed from the bottom of Roan Mountain where it feels like summer.

Ok, maybe a warm spring.

The trail goes up, and keeps going up.

Climbing is strenuous enough that I don't notice the temperature change. Rocks are frozen over, snow is everywhere and icicles hang from tree limbs. Despite the beauty the climb has me wishing the day was over. I just want to be at the shelter.

The cold shelter.

Over the top of the mountain I'm wondering if I'll ever find the shelter, if I could even keep on going if I wanted to attempt getting off the mountain before dark.

Inside the shelter Padawan sits alone in the dark.

He is done for the day, the climb did him in.

If he's staying I'm staying. Not like I had ever really planned to keep moving anyway. This was it, do or die.

How cold could it really get anyway?

Some women come into the shelter to boil water and cook dinner, away from the wind. It is no warmer inside than it is outside but it makes lighting the stove a hell of a lot easier. When they see me making a cold protein shake they offer the use of their stove.

"Haven't had boiled water the whole hike," I say, "why start now?"

They look at me with pity, or maybe it's something else.

If only they knew I just dumped ice cold water inside my shoe by accident they might have questioned my sanity, or at least my abilities as a hiker. I had been trying to filter water and was shaking so bad from the cold, my fingers unable to make a tight fist that, well, I let the platypus slip from my fingers. It curled over and in slow motion I watched as the freezing spring water poured out of the bottle and into my shoe.

Dumbass.

You're going to lose your toes because you're an idiot.

Climb to the upstairs part of the shelter thinking that somehow the limited space will help it warm up a bit more than downstairs. An older hiker is up there with a look of absolute terror on his face. He wants to keep hiking, get off the mountain before it gets dark, before it gets cold. Only he isn't sure he has enough time.

I put on every piece of clothing I have in my pack, which isn't much. I throw the reflective bivvy around my sleeping bag and unroll my homemade garbage bag tent to lay down on the plywood floor under my sleeping pad. I'm wearing my rain pants for the first and only time of the hike.

Wake up shivering, feeling the cold deep inside is never very pleasant. Without a watch, or the desire to dig around for my cell phone I had no way of knowing if the night was almost over or if it had just began. It had been so cold that there was nothing else to do but climb in the sleeping bag and daydream.

There wasn't a sound that could be heard inside the shelter and it was so dark that it was hard to tell if my eyes were open or not. Usually at least one of the hikers is snoring, or at least breathing heavily, only now there was nothing. Everyone was probably awake, laying there staring off into the darkness praying for the night to end.

Deep breath, filtered through the sleeping bag to stop the biting cold air from going directly into my lungs and I give gtummo another try. Meditate on the flame, relax, and easily fall back asleep.

The next time I open my eyes the sunlight is pouring through the window. Not the kind filtered through gray clouds or thick mountain fog. Clear, radiant sunlight that gave the day hope.

The shelter is still so cold that it is hard to even begin to think about moving. I make my plan, step by step, of what I'll have to do. What gets packed where, and how to get out of there as quickly and efficiently as possible. I try to take an ibuprofen but the water is all frozen solid. Moving breaks a layer of ice off of my bivvy, formed by the condensation from my breath.

Outside it hurts to walk. My ankles don't want to bend, my toes went from being numb to painful. The fingers of each hand hurt to the touch. Down to Carvers Gap hoping I'll eventually warm up, regain some flexibility. Then it's all snow across the windy balds but at least the climbing gets my blood pumping a little and warms me up.

Despite the cold I have to stop frequently to take pictures of the amazing landscape. Then it's left down a hill over rocks and frozen puddles. Warmer, little by little with the incremental change in elevation. The sun slides a little higher and the snow starts to melt. Slowly, wet clumps of snow start to fall from the tree branches high above me.

I taste the snow and realize that I have been running on 20 oz. of water in the last 40 hours. A little gritty but it is cool and refreshing.

Trail Days

Crossing the Tennessee/Virginia border pain shoots up my left foot with every step. I'm sweating more than the heat can account for and I find myself holding my breath for extended periods of time to fight back the pain.

It had started Sunday, my one month anniversary of being out on the trail.

We had zero'd at Kincora.

Pix, Padawan and I while Neon Mud and Too Heavy had decided to push on. Only Pix is antsy, she needs something to do, keeps wondering aloud if maybe she should have kept hiking. So we borrow one of the day packs and hike out to Laurel Fork Falls for the view. Only Pix is a runner, and with the light day pack she wants to run.

And it feels fantastic, to move fast, 10 or 15 pounds is infinitely better than 30 dragging you down. And so after the falls, after we get back to Kincora and boredom starts to set back in, I'm not really sure how the idea first came about, the idea of running to Damascus.

Forget the whole crawl to Damascus thing, getting there at the right time so as to enjoy everything but not stay too long, that idea was out the window.

There it was, out for discussion, running to Damascus.

Two marathons in two days.

A quick look at the companion showed Iron Mountain Shelter smack dab in the middle. 25 miles each day didn't sound all that impossible.

Then word starts to spread through the packed hostel, we're RUNNING to Damascus, and everybody has an opinion.

"You'll damage something and be off the trail."

"Is it really worth it?"

"It sounds stupid to me."

Luckily much of the discussion centered around Pix, anytime someone asks me about running to Damascus I casually drop the word running and mention that "We're *hiking* only 25 miles a day. People hike that all the time, what's the big deal."

Granted I had never hiked that far before, let alone two days in a row but they didn't have to know that.

We prep our packs to be shuttled ahead to Mt. Rogers Outfitters, set the alarm for 6:30am, and then lay awake in bed staring at the ceiling.

Listening to everyone downstairs and trying to remember everything, anything I had ever heard about marathon running. Because despite what I had been saying we were planning to run the whole damn thing.

Let's see, marathon running...

Load up on carbohydrates the night before, too late for that. Vaseline between your toes to prevent blisters, no thanks. Multiple socks to start, removing a layer as your feet start to swell into the run? Ok, I could try that.

Not being a runner I didn't know what to expect effort or muscle wise. Shouldn't you train for these things? Laying awake in my bunk I thought, "Aint nuthin to it but to do it."

Besides what could possibly go wrong?

We were up before the alarm clocks. Somehow, between us the idea had changed, Damascus in less than 24 hours. Night hike and it's only slightly more than 2 miles per hour. That's how you rationalize it.

"Don't even think about looking at the waterfall," I say when we hit the trail running. Only it isn't the trail, it's the camping area. A hiker packing up his tent points us in the right direction.

"The trail is over there," he says pointing to a small path leading away from his tent site.

We laugh, giddy with excitement, trying to go fast but still not sure where to go. Through the trees, and back on the trail we push a moderate comfortable pace.

Don't push it. Pace yourself.

The slack pack is so light, 10 pounds maybe a little more, we are bouncing, bounding down the trail over rocks and roots. Then it seems like only seconds later we're at the rock stairs leading down to the waterfall and Pix says she has to stop and go to the bathroom.

Over the sound of the falls I think I hear her say to keep going so I continue to walk/jog at a leisurely pace so she can catch back up.

This'll be more fun with someone to run with.

I pass people just waking up, getting out of their tents. I pass Padawan who left long before us.

"Was hoping to get to Damascus before you guys just so I could flip you the bird," he says as I pass. I walk with Padawan for a while waiting for Pix to catch up, but she doesn't show and Padawan is getting sick of catching all the spider webs draped across the trail.

"Go on Speedy."

I pass and the climb is almost over. Where is Pix? She should have caught me by now, she's the runner after all. Then the trail starts heading downhill and I pick up speed. Faster and faster downhill scanning the ground 5 feet in front of me. Faster and I'm scanning 10 to 15 feet out to make sure there is nothing to trip over.

Scan the trail, check the horizon then back to immediately in front of me. My eyes make the same scan over and over as I run downhill, avoiding loose rocks and protruding roots. I leap over or swing through blown down trees that haven't been cleared yet.

It's the wilderness version of parkour.

Pure running bliss.

The disappointment sinks in at the bottom of the hill. Not only because the rush of speed is over but because the trail isn't clearly marked. The horses behind the fence across the road aren't very forthcoming as to the right direction.

At the lake it seems a little confusing again but by the time I reach Watuga Lake Shelter I check my clock, 2 hours and 40 minutes since I left Kincora.

Where is Pix? Should I wait here? Will she stop at this shelter just off the trail or will she run past without either of us noticing?

Just run my brain says, this feel great.

Then it's the sound of birds in the trees, my labored breathing, in and out of my lungs, and the liquid pressurized sound of my heartbeat in my ears. Pounding. Climbing yet another hill and I start to think about hikers ahead of me, hikers who aren't as strong, that don't deserve to be ahead of me.

I think about catching up to them, coming up behind them fast and leaping onto their backs and tearing into their soft necks with my teeth and ripping the flesh away in a spray of blood as I ride their falling body to the ground. Snapping their spine with my knee as I push their skull into the ground and quickly moving on further up the trail.

God, running is awesome, why haven't I done this before?

By the time I reach Vandeventer Shelter, almost 18 miles from Kincora I'm out of water. Which might have been fine if I had thought to pack my companion along on this little run, but without the guidebook I have no idea where, or even if there is a water source here. There is no mention in the shelter register and there are no apparent signs.

Staring at the Bob Peoples graffiti I try to remember if it was 100 yards north, or south on the trail. Was it that dried up stream bed?

Bob Peoples hunts Chuck Norris for sport.

"C'mon Bob, give me a hint."

When Bob Peoples stays in this shelter the mice bring him food.

"How about the water Bob?"

Bob Peoples gives his boots blisters.

I slow down the pace a little trying to keep my eye out for water, asking hikers about water sources they may have passed.

"Maybe a mile down the trail, on a blue Blazed side trail."

They offer me some of their water but, "It's only a mile." I tell them and quickly take off again.

Then I hit something hard under the leaves covering the trail and a shock runs up my leg, into my thigh. Slowing down everything seems all right, there is no tension. No pain. I decide to take it slow and another two miles up the trail I pass a mother and daughter hiking south.

"Another mile and a half." They tell me in regards to the nearest water.

"Great," I say trying to keep it upbeat, my throat already parched and dry.

Two very thirsty miles later I stumble upon a few thru hikers that I recognize, including a surprised Neon Mud who can't believe that I caught up to him.

"You're a day hiker now?"

I drink water and make even more Gatorade trying to explain the slack pack situation. Neon Mud doesn't want to hear it and takes off down the trail heading for the next shelter, saying goodbye to the thru hikers, and the day hiker (me).

"If you pass me I might throw a rock at you."

I wait there for Pix another 20 minutes before deciding to start walking to the next shelter. Most likely she would wait for me if the roles were reversed. But then again I don't know, we really don't know each other too well, other than where were from and the fact that we are both attempting a thru hike.

She shows up as I arrive at the next shelter, her plan has changed. She wants to be in Damascus by midnight. I'm still thinking 24 hours would be impressive especially when my limp is noticeable when we head out, my lower calf is killing me.

She starts to jog and I try to keep up. She seems mad at me and takes off like she wants to leave me behind. For 4 miles I keep up the pace, landing my foot just right to minimize the pain, until it becomes unbearable and I fall behind.

And then the best Trail Magic happens. Grilled Bacon Cheeseburgers with BBQ sauce at the road crossing, free soda, I'm in heaven sitting in the grass and don't want to stand up or walk ever again.

Pix doesn't want to wait for a burger, she wants to be in Damascus now. I wish her luck, I want her to make it, and she is gone. I take a second, greatly appreciated burger from Forest, a former thru hiker. There is no way you can repay this kind of offering, except by doing Trail Magic yourself.

Leaving hurts. I cross the road limping, following the crushed rock path across the open field, afraid to sit on the bench and enjoy the view as I might not ever start walking again. I may as well be crawling at this point.

Neon Mud who was also slowed down by the Trail Magic was quickly moving off ahead of me, maybe just to prove a point. It's another three miles to the next shelter and I consider sleeping in the abandoned barn in the field, giving up for the night. Only I can't let Neon Mud beat me to Damascus, so I continue to limp along trying in vain to catch up.

I sleep at Double Springs Shelter with Neon Mud, waking up in the middle of the night, knowing that I still had enough time to get to Damascus in under 24 hours. I check my calf and ankle, the pain is there but not bad. I could make it.

"You're going to attempt a painful night hike?" My brain asked.

Nope. I roll over and try to sleep, the failure of making it in 24 hours weighing heavily on my mind.

So, packed full of ibuprofen I crossed the Tennessee/Virginia border. Despite the limp and the pain and the sweat blurring my vision I was still trying to hurry so no one would pass me on the trail. Neon Mud wasn't going to beat me into town, nothing personal.

The trail runs right through the center of Damascus and recognizing a few hikers they point me in the direction of the Place, a hostel provided by the Damascus First United Methodist Church. Walking in the door I realize that I missed my 24 hour goal by only 4 hours.

Loser.

I grab an empty bunk upstairs and notice Pix in the room across the hall. She only got in a little while ago having had some problems on her run after leaving the trail magic.

It started when she passed a van parked at one of the road crossings. She thought the van was empty until she heard a guy inside yelling, "Shut up! If you don't shut the fuck up I'll kill you!" With no one else around she thought it prudent to take off at full speed, out of the gap, which meant running uphill which quickly tired her out.

By that time it was dark and she was running with her headlamp aimed at the ground in front of her. Only she caught sight of a skunk in the trail and instead of being scared off it ran straight at her. She started yelling and slapping her trekking poles together but to no avail, it kept coming. So she did the only thing she could think of to do and turned around, running back down the trail the way she had come.

By the time she thinks she lost the skunk she turns around to see that it is still coming towards her. She runs more but it doesn't do any good. She drops branches and tree limbs across the trail trying to divert the skunk. It just climbs over and keeps coming. This time she jumps off the trail into the woods climbing downhill. That's when her headlamp decides to go out.

In the dark, 25 feet off the trail she listens for the skunk but doesn't hear anything. She waits for a while before climbing back up to the trail and makes her way to Queens Knob Shelter, one of the oldest shelters on the AT and intended for emergency purposes only.

She figured this might count.

Meanwhile The Place is amazing. No one seems to work there, the rules are posted on the wall and people move through the house, each doing their own thing. Microwaving dinner in the tiny kitchen. Waiting for one of the showers to open up. Pulling impossible amounts of gear out of packs stuffed like clown cars. People lucky enough to have scored a ride to Food City for resupply carry large bags back to their bunks, some of it they repackage, a lot of it is to eat immediately.

Baltimore Jack is at Mt. Rogers Outfitters answering phones and questions from hikers. He points me to a back room filled with mail drops to get my now seemingly oversized pack. I browse their inventory thinking about downsizing.

I spend the next two days being lazy, eating pizza, blogging, uploading pictures and videos to try to and keep friends back home up to date with the hike so far. Pix, Padawan and Too Heavy work out at tent city clearing areas for the incoming hikers, and there are a lot of incoming hikers. Not only are all the bunks full at the Place but people are staking out floor space and the yard is wall to wall tents.

There is something going on for hikers all the time, between all the churches and gear sponsors there are showers, hiker feeds and stuff you wouldn't believe, foot massages? Really?

Then the five of us are all out at tent city with our own little group area. Pix's friend has come in to start hiking with her making six of us. Freyr and a few others join us in our circle and it feels like home, more than home has in a long time, maybe ever.

Then we start drinking.

After that it's all a blur.

A long painful blur which at times makes me feel like I was hit in the kidney with a baseball bat. It hurts to move, but I was so drunk I have no idea how I got so hurt.

It all comes back in flashes. Flashes that make me giggle, flashes that make me feel ashamed.

Rumors of arrests, a police sweep through town, cops or informants dressed all in black hiding in the trees watching hikers for illegal activities.

Damascus General Store across from tent city, racks of sodas, that fresh wood smell when you walk in, Pix telling me that there were two kinds of birch beer, red and white. Sioux City birch beer is red, and damn good.

A Backpacker Magazine drawing in which I won a pair of Leki Trekking poles. Spending way to much at Mt. Rogers Outfitters on a new, smaller backpack and sleeping pad.

Walking in the 25th anniversary Trail Days parade, squirt guns, water balloons, a guy with a gun in his belt on main street antagonizing hikers and being antagonized relentlessly in return.

Deep fried Oreo's.

And then I was alone.

Standing in the woods behind the baseball diamond watching my unread magazine smolder in the ashes of last nights fire. The coals still hot as rain drops penetrate the canopy above. A last long look at the dry spots that were recently covered by tents and tarps, and it is time to move.

Reluctantly shouldering my new pack I dread walking the 20x12 tarp, a bag of garbage and my old pack stuffed full of my tent and other assorted gear back into town. I'm the last one, everyone else has left ahead of me, heading back to the trail, except Pix and her friend who are doing Hardcore, a volunteer trail maintenance thing with Bob Peoples.

Back to town through the mud and drizzle. The hitch is easy, back of a pickup truck with a hiker I have never met before, it starts to rain.

"Maybe this was a bad idea." She wonders, looking up at the gray skies.

I've never seen her before, probably never see her again. The trail is like that, people only days ahead of me will never be seen, people behind me will never catch up.

There are only three tents left in the yard next to the Place. Inside people are repairing gear, getting ready to hit the trail. Bunks are becoming available and with the rain I don't really feel like moving on just yet.

Then I realize that I have just spent an entire week in Damascus.

Damascus Suck

I pack and ship my Osprey Talon 44, sad to see it go, excited about the new smaller backpack. The Osprey Hornet 32 is packed with the usual gear plus 15 pounds of food and ibuprofen. Too much food, I had tried to give some away, dropped some in the hiker box at the Place. I had put my tent in there and it disappeared almost instantly. Turns out people linger there waiting for the departing hikers to drop stuff and they scoop it up.

Lurking, pouncing like hungry vultures, not because they need the equipment, but so they could sell it.

Out of town on the Creeper Trail and up into the woods where I unload the Leki poles and give them a try. Reluctant to leave town at first it now feels good to be back in the woods, to be moving again.

I wonder about getting blisters on my hands from using the walking poles. I worry about aerating the soil with the tips, contributing to soil erosion along the trail, vaguely concerned about stabbing the roots of living trees as well.

I almost trip myself once, then stab myself in the leg further down the trail, but I seem to be moving faster. The lighter pack I wonder, then I'm back down to the Creeper Trail again. Turns out a lot of people leave Damascus drunk or hungover and skip the little part of the AT that leaves the Creeper Trail.

They are literally "creeping" out of Damascus.

The trail was originally part of the AT so they aren't cheating they claim, retro blazing it's called. They get so used to walking the Creeper Trail that they miss the AT turnoff after the bridge and keep going, one couple did 6 miles before they realized they were no longer on the Appalachian Trail.

I worry about making it to Lost Mountain Shelter having ditched both my tent and tarp in town. I need the shelters now, until I can pickup the smaller tarp in a mail drop

A thru hiker on the side of the trail is holding his stomach when I walk up.

"Giardia," he says, "Probably have to go back to town."

For a moment I'm torn, I want to help him but can't think of anything to do short of walking him back down the trail. He says he'll be fine and I start moving, fast. I pass 11 other hikers and hope there aren't too many others between me and the shelter.

When I get there three people stand around talking, two have already set up in the shelter, the third just started the trail today and wants to keep going. All the hikers I passed and a few extras start showing up, 9 of us are packed in the shelter meant for 8, a dozen or so tents are spread out in the surrounding woods.

Another 10 or 12 hikers moved on to a campsite a mile up the trail.

Around the campfire I notice that my left lower calf is hurting and is swollen, it hurts to lift the toes and bend my ankle.

Problems from taking a week off in Damascus?

The two that were here first are teachers from a sociology group, they were part of a larger group but the rest of them gave up and went into town for real food and warm showers. After only one night out on the trail even the two that stayed here are second guessing their decision.

Rain and cold. I wanted to sleep in so bad but I had to get ahead of all these people, to get to the next shelter to insure that I had a spot. Not just the next couple of nights either but for the next week. My mail drop miscalculation was sure to be a disaster.

I skip breakfast, should at least eat some peanut butter I'm thinking but other people have already left. I move fast with the poles but I can tell after only a day that my shoulders are adjusting to the new workout.

Originally I had wanted to take it slow through Grayson Highlands, a highlight of the hike everyone had agreed. Only the lighter pack hasn't made me want to enjoy the trail anymore, it makes me want to go farther, faster. If another hiker is visible ahead of me on the trail it becomes an obsession to pass them. If I just passed another hiker I can no longer think about stopping to eat or refill my empty water bottle.

Not that I should do either of those things if I haven't done at least 12 to 15 miles anyway.

Hiking into Thomas Knob Shelter I started thinking maybe take a break, have some lunch, some ibuprofen, there were a couple of spaces still left in the shelter, maybe I'll stay. Then a handful of people finished their lunch and packed up to hit the trail.

"Put in a few more miles for the day," one of them said.

I look at the hiker curled up in the corner from being kicked by a horse as the words bounced around my skull, a few more miles.

It was too much, my brain wasn't even working, without thinking I packed up and bolted out of there, back on the trail obsessed with passing them. A quarter mile away I realize that I have left my new trekking poles behind.

A quarter mile and I'm not sure if I should go back for them.

Shit.

On the way back I pas more people who had left behind me.

Shit.

"Forgot something?" Another thru hiker asks.

"Just my poles," I say trying hide the fact that all I want to do is run back down the trail.

It takes longer to catch up and pass the people than I thought it would. Every second my mind is racing, go faster, why haven't you passed anyone yet. Then after, why didn't you just play it smart and stay at Thomas Knob?

Why are you rushing?

I don't know.

"That's a real teeny pack you got there," a hiker comments as I pass her.

"Stripped the gear down to bare bones," I mention, leaving her behind.

"Guess you have to keep moving to stay warm?" I hear her say to my back.

Consumed by moving faster, not realizing that she may have wanted to talk I say, "Yep," and keep moving.

I understand now what Almond meant in Hot Springs when he said he was trying to slow down but just didn't seem to be able to. Being light is an addiction, an addiction that requires speed.

Horses try to kick me as I pass them on the trail. I hear hoof beats behind me and I turn ready punch a charging horse or swing my poles in it's direction.

The trail up and over Mount Rogers was anything but a straight line, it was more like a bad lover I kept thinking, cold and it just lays there making you do all the work.

And when you get on top they start crying.

It could have started raining anytime on the hike up, I was hot and sweating and the canopy of leaves overhead would have stopped a lot of it from getting to me. As soon as I break through the cover of trees, it starts raining.

The new pack doesn't have a liner yet, I sent that home too. Without waterproof protection for my sleeping bag I'm wondering if this is going to the coldest most dangerous night of the hike.

Finally Wise Shelter comes into view and my heart sinks when I realize that there are 10 people already there and the shelter holds 8. I ask if they have room anyway, prepared to hike on.

"We aren't staying, we've only hiked 5 miles today and want to keep moving." One of them tells me.

Only the acid they dropped isn't motivating them to keep moving.

They try to get a horse high by blowing smoke in it's face repeatedly. They are feeding the horses anything they can find, pop tarts, Chex mix, spicy gorp. Two of them move on and it becomes apparent that the rest are in for the night. I quickly set up my sleeping pad and bag to insure I have at least some space.

My sleeping bag is still dry but my sweatshirt packed at the top of the bag is heavy with rain water. I hang it up to air out not hoping for too much.

The cold starts to move in and I switch to long johns, dry socks, a hat and gloves. It's too cold to go down to the water. From inside my sleeping bag I eat some peanut butter and wish it was later in the evening, I wish they had moved on or at least made their minds up earlier so I could have gotten ahead of them.

Only the next shelter is probably full too. People keep showing up, some tent even though you aren't supposed to when they realize that the shelter is more than full.

Someone breaks out a radio and they start to get high, "Safety Meeting" is the code word on the trail.

Heads in feet out. I didn't want one of the horses to smell the sweat in my hair and start munching on it while I was sleeping. Everyone seems to agree. No one bear bags, the food is all hung inside the shelter.

Goliath, the hiker packed into the shelter next to me, almost on top of me, is up most of the night puking. From the canned ham he says but a couple of the other hikers ate it too and they aren't sick. Since they left Damascus they have only done 4 or 5 miles a day and despite puking all night Goliath is determined to do 30 miles the next day to get to Partnership Shelter.

Like everyone else he wants to get there for the famous pizza delivery, that and the fact that it has a shower. His plan is to take a zero there. Everyone else seems to be going to the hostel in Troutdale and it is so tempting, warm bed, indoors, soda, maybe a cheese burger.

Out here everything is cold and everything is wet.

I don't own anymore clothes to put on and when I stop hiking the cold creeps back into my toes.

The road to the hostel is only 5 miles away, downhill, and there might even be a shuttle. But I'm trying to slow down to time my arrival so I can pick up my mail drop with the tarp. No matter how I look at it I'll arrive on Sunday, and you can't get mail drops on Sunday.

But without a cell phone signal for the last few days I don't even know if the damn thing was sent, I could be slowing down for no reason, and slowing down will make me miss the hiker feed this Saturday, which really hurts more than anything else.

Despite the cold the hiking is beautiful. The fog was thick most of the day and hanging in the trees it gave the woods a mystical quality. Down the trail through large boulders it starts raining a few times. Not heavy enough to penetrate the leafy canopy, just enough to enjoy the relaxing sound of it's pitter patter on wet leaves.

I can barely make out Goliath ahead of me who seems determined to push his 30 miles, and I hope he makes it.

At Hurricane Mountain Shelter I realize that Freyr and Neon Mud are only a day or two ahead of me. Slowing down will only widen that gap. Knowing Neon Mud he probably pushed straight for Partnership Shelter. I wanted to be there tomorrow but with all the people at the Hostel they have a 5 mile head start on me.

My brain doesn't seem to be working I realize after noticing that I had been sitting at the picnic table shivering in the cold for almost an hour. I'm not going anywhere. I unpack my sleeping gear, clip my toenails and stare off into space some more.

I'm freezing and it's only 3pm.

My new wool socks are already worn through and I notice what looks like a blister forming on the back of my heal. The cuts from the socks I started with had healed there and formed a callus which had worn through the socks like sandpaper. The blister forming there where the cuts had been is warm to the touch and painful. I'm out of water and not motivated enough to go get any so I skip the idea of ibuprofen and just sit there, doing nothing.

The Lazy Boys start to show up. That's my nickname for the guys doing 5 miles a day and getting high most of the time, and they are reading from Lord of the Rings out loud. I fall asleep listening to the story. Someone else is reading from the Hobbit, I didn't know that there were that many books.

One of the girls who just started after showing up at trail days already thinks she has Giardia. They use his phone to access the Wikipedia page trying to diagnose her. A long discussion of poop ensues, color and consistency. They are loud and drop their wet gear right next to my sleeping bag. I'm relieved when they are going to push on, "9 tiny little miles" to Trimpi shelter.

But with the weather a couple of them are trying for the hostel 5 miles away.

No reservations they are told when their call goes through.

One guy flips off his wet backpack cover spraying water everywhere. How can I get away from these guys? First I was going to outrun them, but with the mail drop I gave up on that idea. Slow down and I'm screwed tomorrow. By then they'll all be at Partnership Shelter, so if I cut tomorrow real short and only do the 9 tiny little miles to Trimpi I can slowly let them slip forward.

After Bland I can pass them anytime. Maybe, and for a minute I start thinking about yellow blazing north to Bland to pick up the mail drop early.

God Virginia, what are you doing to me? I haven't seen the sun since I left Damascus.

I'm woken up in the middle of the night from a sharp pain in my heel. The stabbing pain is in the swollen and warm blister. Sleeping in the shelters is hard on your hips and shoulders, even your knees, but never my heels. Without a full length sleeping pad my feet are sometimes subject to cold, but this sharp pain was something different.

Awake in the middle of the night I start to wonder what the hell I am doing. 500 miles into the hike shouldn't I know why I am doing this? It's a different feeling from the beginning of the hike where I would wake up and wonder where I was, or when it was so dark you couldn't tell if your eyes were open or closed.

There is a real uncertainty about what I'm doing. Even the brave voice that says to push on is enfeebled by the fact that I have yet to cover even a quarter of the trail. I had my vacation, I got away from work and home for a while, why don't I call it quits?

Go home for the summer, make some money, go to the beach.

Plan for the next adventure.

Then I'm up before everyone else in the shelter and quietly pack and move out without breakfast. My right heel is swollen and red, the part that bothers me is the small amount of black I can make out underneath.

It hurts to walk. The sneakers are putting pressure where the cuts had been before and where the "blister" is now. I'm not so sure it is a blister anymore, it's like something is inside, infected and inflaming my heel to three or four times it's normal size.

I try to ignore it.

5 miles to Dickey Gap. Maybe a hitch to resupply. Not that I need it, I just want a Coke so damn bad.

Between the pain in my heel and the poles I quickly start to lose my mind.

It's so simple really, the poles keep stabbing the leaves on the ground. The leaf, or two or three will get stuck to the bottom and I would watch it, moving with me until I had to shake it free. Or worse try to get the leaf free by using the other pole, all the time not looking at the trail or where I was going. If I had to stop to remove the leaf then the poles really weren't making the hike any faster.

"What do you want to do, collect leaves or hike?"

I feel like a prisoner in an orange jumpsuit on the side of the highway. I wanted to smash them against a tree.

"One week," I said out loud, "if you make it to Troudale, I'll give you one week to prove yourselves."

At Dickey Gap I try to will the entire force of the universe into making a ride appear. I wait all of 30 seconds before deciding that it didn't work and start limping up the road. Just then an old converted ambulance drives up, Gary the driver is shuttling hikers up and down the trail trying to score beers and some spare cash. If I had just waited a minute more and had a little faith the ride would have appeared.

I'll have to remember to try that again in the future.

Sitting in the restaurant I notice for the first time just how much I smell. I try to make a call to verify my mail drop even got sent but the whole town is a dead zone another thru hiker tells me between mouthfuls of his ham and cheese omelet. The sociology teachers are there having yellow blazed down from Thomas Knob Shelter.

Out here the conversation revolves around the weather, not in a polite, you have nothing else in common to talk about kind of way, but in a real way. The weather has real meaning when you spend all of your days and nights out in it. At the restaurant voices hush and conversations come to a halt when the weather report comes on telling us about an upcoming break in the bad weather.

Why do short days in the woods when I can have a shower and let my heel heal?

I'm at the hostel run by the Troutdale Baptist Church before I can talk myself out of staying.

In the bunk room I try to drain some of the fluid from my "blister". The swelling seems to have come down a little and I manage to drain the smallest amount of blood and white blood cells. It's too painful to touch and suddenly I am very tired and a chill enters my bones.

I start to shake convulsively from the chill. So cold. I try to crawl into my sleeping bag to warm up but nothing helps.

"Holy shit is hot in here," another hiker says coming into the room, "aren't you hot enough?"

"I'm fucking freezing," I say, "But you can turn it off, I think somethings wrong with me."

He reluctantly shuts it off and goes back to whatever gear problem he was having. I try the Tibetan gtum-mo practice to build up some internal heat only there is no little flame to start visualizing with, my torso is a cold empty shell. I try again and again to get some sort of flame visualization going and it is harder than ever. When a flame does appear it is different, thin with oily black smoke coming off of the top.

That's when I remember the story that the disciples of this technique couldn't sleep with covers or too close to a fire. It destroys what they worked so hard for. The shower when I first got here was hotter than anything I had felt in a long time, so hot it was painful to stand under. The little bits of flame flicker and die out as waves of cold surge through my body.

I try again to fall asleep, you're out of your mind, it's a cold, probably from Goliath when he was sick next to you in the shelter, I try to tell myself. Just a cold.

The bunks fill up, people come and go, I sleep for hours. Laying in bed I think about the white blazes. I have to hike past each and every one if I want the completion certificate. But what do I need that for?

The thought leaves me in dangerous territory of skipping a few miles here and there.

I'm only 50 miles out of Damascus and my mind is a mess.

I force myself to get up and get something else to eat. By now all the bunks are full and people are setting up sleeping bags in any available floor space. There are rumors of fights and cops at Partnership Shelter, emotions are flaring up and down the trail, everyone is cold and sick of being wet.

By the time I manage to get back to my bunk I am shivering uncontrollably again. My joints ache and I have no energy. I sleep the rest of the day and at night I get up to sit in the chair in front of the heater. After an hour I realize again that I have been staring off into space not thinking, not moving. I get back into bed and sleep through the night.

In the morning Apex, another thru hiker, apologizes for keeping everyone up all night from puking, he is sick too and everyone else is complaining about low energy levels. I didn't even hear him getting sick.

Surprisingly the fever and chills seem to be gone, the heel is still massively swollen. I decide to coat it with Neosporin and walking seems a little easier. The place empties out and only a couple of the sick hikers and a guy waiting for a mail drop remain behind. They play horse shoes and smoke weed all day.

When it's too dark for that they play Scrabble and listen to a little mp3 player hooked up to a speaker.

I'm in a lazy mood, thinking about the trail, about not hurrying. It's not a race, I don't have to catch up with or pass anyone, not the people I was hiking with, not anyone. Laying in bed the night before I had thought about disappointing work by not finishing early enough. About how I had to skip ahead to get back on track.

Today all of that is gone, sitting in the grass under the sun, listening to neighbors mow their lawn. The hurry, the hustle is fading. Do the trail. Hike my own hike.

Work is not my life.

My heel is suddenly more interesting than anything going on around me. The swelling is down, the red part seems less red, though it has a white center about three inches across and it is purplish underneath. I press it a little to see how tender it is and pus oozes out. I push a little more and a tablespoon full of chunky dead white blood cells squirts out with some blood. I push a little more and the wound foams, like air escaping from inside.

Hopefully that's a good sign.

The hiker feed starts at 6pm and hikers are coming out of the woodwork. Sorry, the signs say Hiker Picnic, feed sounds like everyone has lined up at a trough. On the other hand that's not too far from the truth.

Pix and her friend show up among the others and I'm happy to see her until after the pre meal prayer she blurts out to a table full of people about my ankle. Not just people, church people.

Immediately they are concerned, "You should see a doctor."

"It could spread."

They tell me stories about hikers ending up on crutches or worse, having their legs amputated.

I tell them that I prayed really hard and everything will work out just fine.

"Prayers and means," a lady says, "A means to fix it."

Another lady from the church who you could tell didn't quite fit in said, "When I worked for the Vet they just soaked the animals paws in Epsom salts. Charged people $30 and all I did was hold their paws."

The others look away, obviously not approving of that down home country advice.

I like that idea a hell of a lot more than some antibiotic pill.

The pastor gets everyone's attention and and starts a sermon trying to tie together faith in God with hiking. I quickly lose interest when I realize that the premise of the sermon is that God made us all flawed, programmed to be sinners and break the ten commandments.

"The only way you will know peace is through accepting Jesus."

At least now I know that I'm not Baptist.

Not that I'm ungrateful but that meal felt way too expensive to be considered free.

Virginia Blues

"Any thru hiker that tells you they walked past every white blaze and touched it is a liar," the shuttle driver was saying to a couple of thru hikers that wanted to go back a couple of miles to where they got off trail.

The swelling in my ankle had gone down considerably and I was antsy to get back on the trail myself. Luckily where I got off trail was right down the road, which is where he wanted to drop the other hikers off. One stop, make it easy, then he could go back to drinking.

There is another hiker feed a couple of miles down the trail and I start to wonder why I bothered to resupply. No sermon, not even a prayer this time. In fact they all seemed so shy most us felt obligated to try and start conversations, to tell stories from the trail to keep them entertained.

Then they shuttle us back to the trail and we make the run for Partnership Shelter. Ok, I make the run to Partnership showing up more than an hour before the next hiker behind me.

Hello speed, it's good to be back in the woods.

Everyone at Partnership was already drinking. Hearts and 'Never Have I Ever' games turned into beer shotgunning contests. A former thru hiker had shown up at the shelter in her car and lent it to people to drive into town for a beer and pizza run. It was a full blown party and I wanted nothing more than to keep moving.

The police had been in every night since the end of Trail Days and people were working fast to drink the beer before it could be confiscated. Many of the hikers had caught a ride in from Troutdale, it wasn't about the hike, it was about the moving party.

Like they say, Hike your own Hike.

I slept through most of the off key singing and drunken revelry, and early in the morning crept out of the shelter and down to the dam where Pix had tented with her friend. I wanted to say goodbye because I had a feeling this would be the last time I would see her, except they were still sleeping.

"I'll miss you," I say quietly and move on.

This was the first day of the hike that there was no plan, no idea of where to stop for the night, no idea what I was doing for the day. There was no motivation to hike either, but once started I was glad to be on the move. Without a tarp or tent I really should be making some sort of decision, but I was ready to let the day take me where it wanted, to be fully and completely at the mercy of the trail.

Just white blazes and a long brown winding foot trail covered with last seasons decaying leaves. Green sprouting everywhere and the thickening canopy blocks and filters the early morning sunlight. I'm alone, first one on the trail.

Too bad about all these spider webs.

By lunchtime The Barn Restaurant looks inviting and several hours are spent eating, journaling, making calls home and generally laying in the grass. There's 15 hikers spread out on the grass waiting for a party shuttle, out to some farm, promised by some guy I wasn't sure would follow through. But they wait, the trail is all mine again, and somehow I end up doing over 25 miles for the day at a leisurely pace. I step into Knot Maul Branch Shelter just as the thunder rolls across the sky and the rain extinguishes the fire.

There is a brand new trash bag in the shelter that I can now use as a pack liner.

The trail provides.

Everything is good.

"Guess you're not a thru hiker," the older hiker says while filtering water.

"I am," I say, "started April 8th, how about you?"

This is his second thru hike and he started a week before me. I couldn't imagine why you'd want to do this a second time but didn't ask.

"You have a trail name yet?"

"Cleanshave, because I shave on the trail some people think I'm just a day hiker."

But clearly from the way he was eying my pack he didn't think that was the reason. His own pack must have been about twice the size of mine.

"Don't know what you got in that magic pack but most thru hikers don't have one that small."

I try to explain the gear but he isn't listening, just staring at the pack, lost in his own thoughts.

"It isn't the same this year," he says. "Don't know if it's me, the crowd? It's just not the same."

He looks at me for some insight I am unable to provide.

Why would you want to do this all over again, haven't you seen all this already?

Again I don't ask, instead I offer some useless platitude about having a good hike or keeping a stiff upper lip or maybe you should blow your brains out if your so unhappy.

I forget which.

The rest of the day the thought of hiking all of this a second time keeps coming back. Despite all the great moments, the views, the people, I hate hiking. Really there is no reason for me to still be going, except to finish.

Then what?

For that there is no answer. Not even a spark or faint echo from anywhere in my wildest imagination.

Let's just worry about finishing the hike.

"Why?" a little voice asks quietly somewhere inside my head.

The sky behind me turns dark, there is a big storm brewing near the trail crossing outside Bland. Only there is no sign as to what road you're on or which way to town. A minivan pulls over for my outstretched thumb just as it starts raining, the same time as a group of hikers emerge from the trail. We all cram into the van laughing. The one good thing about hikers is that no matter how bad a day you've had, you always seem to be in a good mood.

Even with all the rain the priorities are the same, gas station for junk food and milk, then post office for the mail drop with the tarp. A few thousand calories later and I'm in no hurry to leave. A bunch of hikers get rooms at the Big Walker Hotel and logically I should just hike the two miles out of town to stay in the next shelter. Instead I split a room with Knotty, a psychotherapist.

I mention this because he has an interesting take on why people attempt to thru hike the Appalachian Trail.

"People are out here to find something, lose something, or a combination of both."

Which on second thought seems to cover just about everything.

The door to our hotel room is wide open, the rain starts again and turns to hail, the skies turn black as night, and for a long while I just stand there in the doorway. Nothing to do, not a care in the world.

"I wish I could pack a laptop," I say out loud, to no one in particular.

"What for?" Knotty asks.

"To get some work done."

"Work? This is supposed to be a vacation."

It's supposed to be, for everyone else. I'd like to be working, bringing in some money to make sure I can finish, to make this a lifestyle not a vacation. I pull a chair out front of the hotel and watch the highway. I could stay here for a month, just like this, and watch the world go by.

The next day I try to find any excuse not to leave. I want time to freeze, to be suspended in this moment for all of eternity. But it can't happen, or at least it doesn't. Time keeps on ticking, entropy creeping in through the edges.

"Hey, do you need a ride back to the trail head?" a voice behind me calls out.

I don't even have to hitch out of town, rides fall out of the sky.

"Save money. Get out of town," my brain says.

From the trail head I hike all of two miles to the first shelter and just sit there, staring off into space. Staring at the thru hiker companion. Doing nothing.

In the morning I feel better. Time to start moving.

I cruise down the trail, starvation training. No food, no water until I've done at least ten miles.

Also known as Fasted Training, avoiding carbs before and during a workout converts fat to fuel more efficiently. Without succumbing to the craving to eat I should be able to maintain blood sugar levels for longer amounts of time.

That's my half assed theory anyway.

Despite having shipped my sleeping bag home to save a few pounds it felt like I wasn't getting anywhere. I kept walking but it felt like I was doing it in slow motion.

Like the air was made of Jello.

Randomly thoughts would pop into my head, old memories of events or situations that would make me embarrassed or ashamed.

The time I told my ex-girlfriend on the phone that I liked the song Jessie's Girl, she was so weird then hung up after that, only then did I realize that her new boyfriend's name was Jessie.

The time I had met an old friend at a bar after not seeing them in years. We drank too much, 25 cent buffalo wings being forced on me, drunk driving to his house where he backs into me at a red light and I'm so drunk I think maybe my brakes didn't work. He is laughing like a madman and drives away, I have to push the pedal to the floor to keep up.

Drag racing shit faced.

At his house, white shag carpet, white leather couch, I projectile vomit red and orange buffalo wing sauce over everything.

Then leaving having no idea where I was, driving in ever widening circles looking for something familiar.

The time I pulled a gun on that guy behind the church intent on shooting him dead for making fun of my shorts.

I was visibly cringing and reacting to the thoughts as if they were happening in the current moment. I had to stop an make sure no other hikers were around to see my antics.

The memories were too much, like deep seated poisons working there way to the surface, and without a better idea I decided to burn them.

I would take whatever image my memory had served up and set it on fire Bright orange and yellow flames would consume the memory with a whoosh. The picture would turn various shades of gray and crumble into ashes that would break apart into a fine powder and drift behind me as I walked.

As I continued to walk the microscopic ashes were left far behind. Once this started all kinds of memories, from the mildly embarrassing to the downright prosecutable would offer themselves up for the flame.

After several hours of this my walking slowly lightened up and my step seemed a little quicker.

By the time lunch rolled around I felt downright peaceful. A quick bite to eat at Seeley-Woodworth Shelter and I came across an entry that sort of spoke to how I felt, how many of the thru hikers must have felt at this point.

"Don't know what I'm getting out of the trail anymore."

The hiker went on to say that they were going to zero and try to figure out why they should keep hiking. The last part of the entry stuck with me though, *"Not down,"* they said, *"Just unsure."*

If it wasn't for the fact that I had nothing to go back to I was sure I'd be in the same boat.

The truth is that I don't know why I'm still hiking. Only now it seems as if I have crossed some kind of threshold, that anything I may have obtained from hiking the trail is now more possible. That all this time out here hasn't been wasted.

It's a test of will.

That thought seemed to temper the peaceful feeling into something new. For the next four miles I don't remember much about the trail. The backpacks stacked around the sign for Spy Rock were the first sign of another hiker all day.

"There's no way they passed me." I thought recognizing a few of the packs.

The Lazy Boys.

Turns out they hitched into Glasgow, then into Buena Vista, then from there they took a bus into Lexington to catch a movie. After that they picked up a shuttle and stayed at the Dutch Haus. They hadn't been hiking since their swim in the James River, 35 miles by trail.

At the Priest Shelter, where tradition is to write some sort of confession in the register Curious George admits that he will no longer say he is a thru hiker. Everyone wonders if that means he is quitting the trail.

"Nope. I'm backpacking from Georgia to Maine. I've yellow blazed enough that I don't want to call myself a thru hiker."

To me the idea that the trail consists of two points, a beginning and an end, wasn't something that I had considered before. How you get from end to end is your own adventure. It doesn't all have to be hiked.

Earlier in the trail when a veteran thru hiker had said to bunch of us around a campfire in Georgia that in his experience, "It didn't matter a damn to the outside world that you hiked the Appalachian Trail, what matters was what your hike meant to you."

I hadn't really grasped the full importance of what he was saying at the time, still wrapped up in wondering what the hell I was doing and the monumental task of finishing on time so I could get back to work. Everybody is out here for a reason, we just don't all know what that is, and each of us deals with that uncertainty in different ways.

I hiked on, by myself, over the Priest with the bugs in my eyes, hair and ears. Swatting at them, trying to wipe the sweat out of my eyes, trying to find decent footing on the loose and jagged rock path. There's blood left behind after I swat at the swarms, my blood. My fingernails are filled with blood and bugs from swatting and scratching. But then the climb is done and it's a full run down the other side, down steep hills and across streams that all feed into Cripple Creek.

I lose my momentum for the day after climbing up the other side of VA 56 and end up staying at Harpers Creek Shelter with a day hiker. He had sent his brother home earlier in the day with knee problems and was trying to hike back to his car. Hes got a big Coleman stove and several aluminum water bottles. The pack is at least 60 pounds with a 4 D cell Maglite on the outside and has to be hoisted onto the picnic table before he can put it on, before he can head out to climb up and over the Priest into the afternoon heat.

He needs to get within cell phone range so he can call his wife and tell her that he's all right. He hasn't been able to call her since yesterday, "She must really be worried."

"She should be, I'm worried you won't survive your little eight mile hike," I want to say, but fuck it, he'll figure it out for himself.

Shenandoah

Waynesboro, VA is too easy.

I cruise the 27 miles from Harpers Creek Shelter to Rockfish Gap. The plan had been to stop over night at the Paul C. Wolfe Shelter but when I hit it by 3pm all I could think about was running. Despite the heat, despite the cool river right in front of what looked to be a nice and spacious shelter, I wanted to keep running.

Anything less than Waynesboro and I'd be a failure.

The trail maintainer had almost killed it for me but I was still too pumped to do anything but keep moving. Sitting around I would just seethe, I would hate myself for relaxing. I had to use that anger, channel it into moving forward.

And it was such a silly little reason to be so worked up.

I had been almost out of water when I passed the maintainer working on clearing the trail. He was smoking a pipe and seemed friendly enough.

"How's your hike going?" He asked.

"Hot, and I'm ready for some water."

"Do you need some?" He asked concerned, only I did have one more sip in my 20 oz bottle, and I can never bring myself to take water from people who have hiked it out themselves. Feels like charity, or welfare.

"Well there's a visitors center about a mile up," he says. "You should be fine."

A visitors center? Water? Soda machines?

This quickens my pace and the next mile is a blur. Then there is a sign, "No Camping, No Campfires" That has to be because I'm close to the visitors center I think and push on. Only there are no side trails, no other signs.

No visitors center.

At an open view area another hiker has stopped for a break. I ask about the visitors center but he hasn't heard of one in this area. He has a rash on his back from his pack and his knee is giving him a hard time.

"Might have to take a couple of zero's in Waynesboro," he says in agony.

I swish the last sip of water around in my mouth to savor it before swallowing.

"So no visitors center huh?" I'm a complete dick, but what am I going to do carry the guy? Besides he is old enough to take care of himself. Anything less is natural selection.

Back up to the Blue Ridge Parkway I spot a rock with water dripping off of it just off the trail at a parking area.

"If it drips, I'll have a sip." Besides which there didn't seem to be any other option.

My heart stops for a minute when I realize that someone has thrown trash into this pristine looking water and the very small pool that has collected at the base of the rock. Then I get closer and realize that someone, probably the trail maintainer that I had been cursing for the last three miles, has put bottled waters, sodas and Gatorade's into the cold puddle.

32 oz Gatorade's, not the smaller ones the trail angels usually provide. And for a minute I'm in heaven. The anger at the trail maintainer being wrong about the visitors center turns into something else. And now, hydrated, I'm ready to hunt and kill the next target.

Waynesboro.

At Rockfish Gap there is a waterproofed list of trail angels willing to provide free shuttles into town, and it turns out there is a cell signal here. The first number I call is answered on the second ring and he says he'll be there in a couple of minutes. Before I can snap a picture and type a caption he has pulled up and is loading my pack into the back of his truck.

"So where to?"

"Lutheran Church?" I ask having heard on the trail that it is one of the better places to stay.

And we're off. Once downtown he turns into a tour guide giving me the layout of the town, pointing out places of interest. The post office, the supermarket for resupply, the library for internet access, and finally the Lutheran Church.

Front door service.

The church doesn't let hikers inside until 5pm, so my timing couldn't have been better. Except that I'm still sweating from having run down to Rockfish Gap and the air conditioning is set to arctic blast. I'm shivering as Collette takes my picture and gives me a name badge before showing me around.

Signs are posted everywhere, don't sleep on the stage, don't do this, don't do that. Only none of them sounds demanding. It's more like they want to remind the hikers to respect that this is a church, and these people couldn't be more accommodating. Showers, TV, computers and free food. Tons of free food.

"Eat anything you want in the refrigerator. Cups and plates are in the cupboards, feel free to use whatever you like," she points out the food leftover from the hiker feed they had the night before, and the milk that needs to be consumed.

Milk? Two gallons of whole milk.

I would have kissed her if it seemed at all appropriate.

I don't know when the thought hits but as soon as it does I know I'm as good as done.

Zero.

Decompress, you're supposed to be slowing down, enjoying this whole thing remember? Nothing to rush back to, no where to go or be by any specific date. Slow down.

And I do, for a whole day.

Then the van drops a crowd of us off back at Rockfish Gap for the hike into Shenandoah National Park. Everyone is goofing off at the registration kiosk and I figure it's time to put a little distance between us, nothing personal, I just didn't want to be hiking in a group.

An hour so later I pass a section hiker heading south, he warns me about the low water levels in the park. No problem, I still have a full 20 oz bottle of water from this morning.

And then I'm cruising again, in the heat, and sweating more than I should have let myself. At a road crossing a trail angel named Bill Gallagher leaves bottled water behind, it's warm but I decide to take advantage of the free 16 ounces of water.

Immediately I feel guilty.

Why are you such a pussy? Drink your own water.

So I run, run right past Calf Mountain Shelter and the last chance to refill my water bottle. Run through what seems to be a continuous uphill climb, past older thru hikers that started a month before me on the verge of dehydration on the side of the trail.

The sky clouds over and maybe because I want it so bad the rain never comes.

Then I'm at Blackrock Hut and the spring has dried up. Every few seconds a drop of water reluctantly falls from the rusted pipe protruding from the stream bed.

"You stupid fuck," I say out loud, laughing at myself.

Luckily a little exploration down the dry stream bed brought me to a few puddles at a bend, under some shade. A little bit farther down stream and the puddles were actually big enough to filter some of the water out.

My problem wasn't the water, it was the urge to keep running. Only 13 miles to the next hut.

"C'mon, you can do it. That's only three or four hours max."

It was early enough, there was plenty of daylight, and I had been thinking of the craziest idea. For the last week or so I couldn't get it out of my head. Run the entire length of the AT through Shenandoah National Park without sleeping.

Run through the night, run all day. Run until I started hallucinating.

The only drawback to that idea was the fact that the park had food available at camp stores and wayside restaurants. As much as I wanted to burn through every part of my body and leave it all here on the trail the thought of eating sounded, well, a little more reasonable.

It was all I could do to sit still and drink another protein shake.

A lot of people take advantage of the waysides and camp stores in the park to go light. Even with the extra food everyone told me I didn't need my pack weight was still only at about 15 pounds. It is pretty cool to come out of the woods and walk right up to a store and buy soda and milk then be back on the trail in a matter of minutes.

The problem is that the food could have been better. First it was out of date milk at both the Lewis and Loft Mountain camp stores. I was hoping for at least a discount then started to get worried that they'd refuse to sell it to me and went ahead and drank it anyway.

Then it costs extra to add cheese to an already overpriced burger, and when I ask for it to be cooked medium the waitress gives me an attitude, "Well done only, park policy."

Then I hear Skyland has a breakfast menu in the Pollack Room. Started out with an omelet and breakfast potatoes. The omelet had no flavor and the breakfast potatoes turned out to be cut up steak fries. Order a stack of buttermilk pancakes to try and fill the hole in my stomach, only they too are flavorless and break apart into mush on my plate.

So disappointing. One of the worst breakfasts I've had, not just on the trail but in my entire life.

I'm trying to sleep but my sister keeps trying to wake me up. I'm in my moms house and she is telling me it's time to go back to work.

"I just got off the trail for Christ sake."

Then annoyed at work interrupting my sleep I try to remember when I got off the trail.

How long has it been?

What was Maine like?

Then I'm awake in the shelter, morning barely cracking over the horizon.

I try to sleep in, letting the other thru hikers get out well ahead of me. Without a sleeping bag it can get pretty cool during the night and sleeping in a little later is a bit warmer. Only I still end up passing them later. When I mention how nice it is to take an easy day I'm surprised by their reaction.

"It's not about the miles, it's about the smiles." Only their tone of voice isn't anything friendly, it's more of a condescending one. Later it occurs to me that maybe they weren't taking it easy, maybe that's as hard as they push themselves.

And then I just feel like a jerk.

Halfway

Then I'm running again.

I can't seem to punish myself enough.

The Roller Coaster is a view-less, 13 mile section of trail everyone had been dreading. It's a series of ten climbs, and after the first climb I'm scoffing at the trail maintainers warning sign. This is nothing, piece of cake.

Then the second hill is a bit bigger and I realize that I'm still not at the top, it keeps climbing, then a little more. Then there's an elevation drop which instead of signaling the end of the climb is a yet another false summit.

And then I lose my count, did I summit 4 or 5 hills already?

Am I halfway done yet?

I pass another hiker struggling up a hill and ask, "How many was that?"

"Six," he says, out of breath. Only I'm dubious. He has to have overestimated how many climbs because he wants to be done. I try not to run ahead of him too fast, except once he is out of view I never see him again.

The climb to Bears Den Hostel never seems to end, but no one is around. I was hoping to score a discarded alcohol stove in one of the hiker boxes but I've had no such luck. Switching from No Cook to hot food sounds interesting and would give me something new to learn.

Finally a lady leans out of the second floor window and tells me the code to the push button lock. Inside is clean and cool and I'd love to stay but it is way too early and I'm still watching my budget. The hiker box is a miss for a stove, cooking cup or even a cozy.

The dilemma starts when I leave. There are cold sodas available, 50 cents each. I have 35 cents. I don't want to leave without a soda, and with no one here...

I hike out to Bears Den Rocks for the amazing view of Shenandoah Valley, without a soda. I can hear the traffic below and I know there is a burger joint down there. I may as well have jumped off the rock ledge for how fast I made it down to the highway.

Only I get lost. And the wind from the passing vehicles is depositing ticks on me at an alarming rate. That's when I realize that the restaurant is not on Va. 7, but on Va. 679. I backtrack over a mile uphill, then downhill to the best burger on the entire AT.

Tracee Wink runs the bar, her two giant dogs roaming the restaurant, decorated with Christmas lights and red topped Formica tables. I take it as a good omen when I notice not only a picture of Edgar Allen Poe but a sign that reads, No Working During Drinking Hours. Beer cans and bottles collected from around the world are displayed on the walls and I can't get enough of the burger and deep fried mushrooms. I'm on the verge of ordering another but a couple locals have offered to give me a ride back up to the trail.

"Oh Hun I can't accept that," Tracee says when I try to pay my bill.

And for a second I actually wonder what kind of hiker heaven have I found that she would give me a burger and soda for free.

Then I realize that the Horseshoe Curve Restaurant doesn't accept plastic, and as I mentioned I have all of 35 cents in my pocket.

"Don't worry Hun, happens all the time."

"Is there an ATM further down the road, maybe I could go get some cash," I ask completely embarrassed.

"No, don't be silly. Here's my card with the restaurants address. You just send me the money when you get it," she says writing my total on the back.

"Happens about every other hiker it seems."

Honestly I'm floored, there is no way anything like that would happen at a restaurant back home. Never. I take the card and leave feeling ashamed. I want to tell her that I promise to mail the money as soon as possible, but words seem so empty for the gratitude that I feel. That she trusts another person, a stranger, this much.

Back on the trail I pass a couple of girls hiking back down to their car.

"Are you heading up to Raven Rock?" they ask.

"Maine," I say feeling confident.

"Yeah, good luck with that," they giggle, rolling their eyes.

So I run, up out of Snickers Gap knowing that I'd be in Harper's Ferry tomorrow. Knowing I had to mail Tracee her cash as soon as possible or I would never forgive myself. There was only one place I had to stop first, the Blackburn Trail Center.

My guide had it highlighted like any other shelter, only the rumor was that it was staffed and they feed you for free. When I came down the hill and saw the extent of the center I figured there was no way this was going to be free.

"Well you're not a thru hiker with that tiny pack..." the caretaker says when she greets me at the door with a cold can of soda.

"Actually I am a thru hiker, just packing kinda light," I say, trying not to sound too frustrated at always having to explain myself.

The soda's free, but there is a suggested donation for dinner. She won't take plastic so again I'm screwed. I promise to sleep on the porch so as not to take up a bunk and skip dinner. Only no one else shows up, just a couple of southbound section hikers that took a zero there.

"Last night we had 25 hikers," she says wondering what she was going to do with all the spaghetti and brownies they made. And so I eat, and it is easily the best spaghetti I have ever had in my life.

The dinner conversation centers around Lyme Disease. The caretaker recently caught it and word had spread up and down the trail.

"It's a different kind of pain or fatigue," she explains.

She is skinny with clear blue eyes and completely harmless, without a hint of anger or regret in her.

"I've been feeling better since the medication. It's not easy," she says catching herself, "Not that my life isn't easy." And she motions to the surroundings, where we are, how she gets to live.

"It's just a lot to deal with."

Does she feel guilty? For living here?

She goes on to explain that this area has the highest rate for Lyme Disease in the country and reminds us to check ourselves often for ticks. The three of us are paranoid after she leaves. Later, trying to sleep in one of the many empty bunks it feels like things are crawling over my skin. I wake up and check with the flashlight but nothing is there.

It rains hard and I plan on sleeping in late. When I finally feel rested enough I pack my bag and check the time, 6:15am. Dammit. I'm already packed so I hike back up to the AT and head for Harper's Ferry.

The trail is jagged and rocky, trekking poles slip and slide off the rocks that pummel and stab the bottoms of my feet. Toes are jammed at awkward angles and there is no time to look up between steps. The landscape is a blur of quartz rocks and unsure footing. The poles are beyond useless and worse, get caught between rocks.

I hate this terrain.

My concentration, focused entirely on the next step causes my mind to wander, almost like my body is on auto pilot. I think about a childrens story I once wrote called The Crown. In it the king travels to far off crusades leaving the princess behind. In the kings absence she throws lavish parties and dances. She grows tired of being the princess and throws her crown out the window of the castle. When the king returns she searches everywhere for the crown but it has disappeared.

I never really had an ending for the story. In fact I wasn't really sure what it meant, except here on the trail it suddenly became apparent that it was about my failure to create an adult relationship. That thing I had passed over, because I didn't commit to a lifelong relationship. I lost out on a part of what it means to be a human being.

From then on I couldn't commit, to anything.

I can see where I failed and how it has affected my life. So I write the end of the story as I hike. In this ending the king is dark and gray, eyes sunken, face like a skeleton as he sits alone on his throne. A chalice in his right hand, "And the king poisoned himself everyday but never died."

After that there were no more adventures for the king, only a blur of monotonous, time consuming, pointless tasks.

Why has it taken me a decade to consider this?

Three large black crows make a racket and follow me down to the Shenandoah River Bridge. They stay in the trees at the edge of the woods and it feels like they are watching me.

Harper's Ferry is the unofficial half way point on the Appalachian Trail. It's tradition to stop in at the ATC office and have your picture taken and get your hiker number. I'm #488 and surprised to see Freyr outside the office getting ready to hit the trail. I had thought he was much farther ahead of me.

"All you ultra lighters should freeze to death," he says when he sees my pack.

It turns out that Neon Mud is coming back to the trail tomorrow after having taken a couple days off here with friends. A few other hikers I knew had given up and gone home. One of the girls had dumped her whole backpack, with everything still inside, in a hiker box and caught a bus to New York.

Even one of the hikers that had been ahead of me by a week is there just signing in and he is surprised when I remember his name. Remember, I think to myself, I think of nothing else but passing you every time I read your name in a shelter register. But I don't tell him this as he is introducing me to his mother, I just wish him well.

That's it, everyone I had been following in the registers is here in town. There is no one left to chase, no one left to hunt down and pass.

My resupply is waiting for me at the post office, it weighs 8 pounds and there is no way I am going to carry that much weight. It gets bounced ahead. The plan had been to come into town, pick up the resupply and quickly leave.

Only now there is a liquor store next to the post office.

And a very clean, quiet hostel just up the hill.

Tending to my feet I realize that not only do my socks smell like a dirty cat litter box, but I have lost the toenails on each of my pinky toes, and another toenail has dug a deep gash into the toe next to it and filled my sock with blood.

No wonder I was limping into town.

After the shower a group of day hikers comes in and wants to talk about their grueling 3 mile hike. They are scrapping plans to do another 3 miles tomorrow because the trail is just too hard on them. Two of them got blisters and are refusing to walk more than necessary. Thankfully there is an expensive restaurant just down the road where they can go for dinner and cocktails.

1,000 miles.

I keep thinking about it over and over. I have hiked over a thousand miles.

That night I dream about my dad's house. He isn't there having passed away over a year before, but the house is filled with clutter. It's his stuff, some of it is mine. It's dusty and things are packed everywhere. My step mom is there wondering what to do with it all and I'm not sure, there is so much it's hard to figure out where to start.

In the morning I can't get my father out of my head.

After that Maryland is packed with day hikers and tourists with water bottles so I'm happy when I finally pass a couple of real thru hikers. Torch and his friend are older and taking it a bit slower.

"Can you tell my wife and daughter I'll be down to the road crossing soon?" he asks when he sees that I am going to speed past them. They had driven down to meet him for lunch at one of the trail crossings.

"Sure, no problem," I say secretly hoping that they'll have brought an extra soda.

At the bottom of the hill there is a sign for Torch pointing up to the parking area. At first I'm reluctant to make the off trail hike, only I had given my word that I would let his family know. And when I find them in the parking lot his wife opens up the back of the pickup truck to reveal bags of food.

"Would you like something to eat?" She asks.

Sodas, Gatorade, homemade baked bread with pepperoni inside, marinara sauce for dipping, baked chocolate covered Saltines.

I eat, trying to control myself. When I get ready to politely leave I'm told to eat more. Another thru hiker shows up and she is trying to show the same respectful restraint. Then three section hikers come up having only been hiking for a couple of nights and finish off everything.

I had wanted to push into Pennsylvania, do a long 40 mile day. The food had a mellowing effect and after only 20 miles I called it quits at the new Ravens Rock Shelter. I was in early enough arriving at roughly the same time as two families out for an overnight hike.

They were tired, their stuff spread out everywhere. They were reading the instructions for their stove trying to figure out how they were going to cook dinner.

"The kids are starving from doing the 6 mile walk in from the parking lot." One of the fathers explains to me.

I check the guide, it's a little over 4 miles, and it took them all day.

The shelter and surrounding area starts to fill up with overnighters and section hikers. When they find out I'm a thru hiker everyone starts coming to me for trail advice. Suddenly I wasn't a lone thru hiker, I was the experienced voice of a long distance hiker. What to eat, what to pack, how to lighten a load, how to hang a bear bag, how many miles, how to purify water. It was more than a little strange, and far from making me feel better it made me miss the company of other thru hikers.

I hadn't been seeing very many.

I hike away from everyone, up a hill to get a cell phone signal. I feel compelled to call my my step mother, we haven't talked since well before my father died, and since the dream about the clutter at my dad's house I have been wondering how she was doing.

There is no answer and I leave a message.

When I get back to the shelter I overhear on of the kids tell his dad Happy Fathers Day.

I didn't know it was Fathers Day.

I also didn't realize what day it was until I saw three of the most beautiful girls walking up the trail.

They were naked and hiking straight towards me.

Hike Naked Day is a hiker tradition and I prayed silently that they would slowly walk by, instead they hustled to get their pull over dresses back on once they saw me. So I did the only thing I could do, I closed my eyes and turned around.

After a decent amount of time I turned back around and they were right in front of me on the trail. Truly three of the hottest girls I could have chanced upon. And they were so clean.

They weren't thru hikers, that much was obvious.

We chat for a little bit but my brain is still mesmerized by the image of them naked, walking towards me. They are so nice and full of smiles I check my hands to make sure I'm not dreaming.

Nope, this is real.

The last thing I want is for them to leave, but I tell them to have fun on their hike and we head off in separate directions. A minute later I turn around and see that they have already stripped off their dresses and for the life of me can't think of a non creepy reason to hike back towards them.

I float down the trail after that, and when an Amish looking hiker is about to pass I greet him with a smile.

"Hello. How are you doing today?"

Only he doesn't respond. And when he gets closer he looks at me with dead gray eyes and says, "What do you want?"

I'm taken off guard by the question but keep smiling.

"How's it going?"

"Nothing. None of your business. Shut up."

And just like that he has ruined what should have been the best experience of the trail. The high that the beautiful girls had provided me with was gone. I was furious. I hiked hard and fast. I hiked angry. I wanted to set the world on fire. I imagined everything burning, everything around me, everything I had ever known or touched. Everything I had ever done, every moment of my life, burnt to a crisp. A dry empty hollow husk of what it had been and then I let the ashes fall to a barren, scorched earth.

In my mind I let my whole body be consumed by the fire. I was no longer hiking made of flesh, my skin was torched, burned into ashes that drifted away leaving only a ghost.

Empty and without substance.

A memory fading with each step.

I kept trying to hike like that, as if I didn't exist. But something primal and deep had been stirred by those naked girls, and now in it's place was a black hate. A hatred so black that the worst atrocities were not only condoned, they were required.

Somehow that blackness was at my core and had survived the the fire that consumed my body.

The hate builds and the trail grows rocky, painful. Boulders and rocks, bugs swarm at my head and fly in my ears and eyes. I feel like a nuclear bomb about to detonate and force myself to stop. The hatred has taken over my hike. I'm blind to my surroundings.

Burn the hate.

I imagine all the blackness as an outfit that I have removed and hold it in my arms. It can't be burned in the usual way, by merely being set on fire. This requires an industrial sized furnace, built from thick wrought iron, ancient and in some deep dark basement.

The garment feels heavy in my hands as I wad it into a ball and feed it into the fire. Close the heavy door to prevent an explosion or contamination. The flames would be too bright. The smoke and ashes are piped out the smoke stack coming out of the top of my head and swirl around me and dissipate as I walk.

I feel quieter now.

There is only the rhythmic click of my poles on the stone and my even, steady breathing.

The sound of traffic is getting close, almost time to eat.

After the BBQ cheeseburger I order a large pizza. When the door opens and the Amish hiker walks in I laugh. He had been lost and going the wrong way on the AT when I saw him earlier. I don't mention how he ruined my day, instead I offer him some of my pizza. He isn't sure, then offers to buy half.

Why not.

"That's the first real pizza I've had in a long time," he says to no one in particular.

Real? The word hangs there for a minute until I realize that he must mean microwaved.

"They try to pass that microwaved pizza off on you at the hostels?"

"Yeah, that's what I meant." And then nothing.

When other hikers come in on a shuttle from a nearby hostel he tries to make conversation, but it is apparent that he has some kind of mental disorder. His statements are strange and vague, when someone asks him a question he gets lost inside his head somewhere.

At the next shelter he lays his sleeping bag right next to mine.

The next day I do 17 miles without water, straight into Pine Grove Furnace State Park for the half gallon challenge.

Eat a half gallon of ice cream in less than an hour to celebrate the real halfway point of your hike.

There is a large crowd of hikers lingering around the store, Neon Mud and Freyr among them. I down a half gallon of cookies and cream ice cream at a leisurely pace of 36 minutes. Freyr manages to slam his down in 22 minutes while several other hikers I have never met can't manage to finish the whole thing in under an hour.

Must be section hikers.

Afterward my tongue starts to thaw out and it feels like it is burning and made of broken glass.

I dream that I'm cooking dinner for a guest. He is in the other room and everything is almost ready. For some reason I have to climb up on the counter and charge a stick in a strange looking outlet that is above the refrigerator.

The stick is about the size of a broom handle but not as long. The end of it becomes charged with static electricity even though I'm having trouble figuring the outlet out. It is as if I've tried the charger before and had trouble, but this time there is no problem.

The stick is to light a fire in the other room where the guest is, only when I try walk on the counter where it rounds the doorway I feel uncomfortable, as if I will become off balance and fall.

The guest in the other room is relaxing and there is no urgency. After a couple of attempts at rounding the corner I decide to climb down from the counter and walk around the corner into the next room, at which point I wake up with a jolt in the dark shelter.

The hike into Boiling Springs is awesome. Across farm land into town and the sound of happy children screaming in a large clear blue public pool. So inviting. I could zero here I think to myself. Along the side of the man made pond, kids feeding ducks with their parents, the elderly sitting on benches in the sun.

I fill my water from a spigot on the back of the ATC office and check the hiker box. Unfortunately I am informed by the volunteers there that a group of Boy Scouts just came through and cleaned everything of value out of it.

I splurge a little and relax with a blue cheese burger and soda at the Boiling Springs Tavern. It's pricey but damn good. Freyr, Neon Mud and a few other thru hikers stagger in out of the hot noon sun. It's comfortable, and instead of leaving by 1 pm like I had planned it is well after 4 pm when I hike out.

The hike out is flat and I cover most of the 14 miles to the next shelter in less than 3 hours. At the end is a climb up to the shelter and the view from the top is stunning. Flat farmland as far as I can see, which could be farther if it wasn't for the massive storm clouds moving in. I wonder if I'll be able to make it to the shelter before the rain, I wonder if Freyr and Neon Mud have even left Boiling Springs yet.

There's plenty of room in the shelter, and the lightning bugs are out. The rain starts, slow at first then pouring, then thunder and lightning close by. Freyr and Neon Mud show up having been only a mile away from the shelter when the worst of it opened up on them. They're soaked.

Freyr hands me a soda bottle filled with Makers Mark whiskey. He doesn't like it. I sip that and watch the lightning bugs in the rain long after everyone has gone to sleep. I listen to the thunder late into the night and think that maybe this is one of the most perfect days of my life.

The next day the hike reminds me of the hike into Damascus.

Painful.

I'm limping and the rocks have done a number on my feet. It doesn't help that there isn't much left to my sneakers. The soles long ago lost any cushioning and now they flap and flail with every step, catching sand and rocks.

Overnight a huge blister has grown somewhere inside my foot on the pad blow my big toe. I pop another ibuprofen and force myself to hike. I keep passing people, and because I just passed them that means that I am not allowed to slow down, so I hike faster, every rock sending a spike of pain up my leg.

"Was that the big climb?" I ask another hiker as I pass. There is only supposed to be one climb for the day and the trail seemed to be leveling off.

"I think it was," he says, except it is soon apparent that he was wrong.

Sweat leaks from every pore soaking my already salt stained shirt. It pools in my eyebrows and drips into my eyes. I try to wipe it away with the sleeve of my shirt, itself already infused with salt from the previous days of sweating.

And the hill keeps going up.

Then there is a sign that says View pointing off off to the right. At a cluster of rocks the breeze is nice after the climb. A German hiker has her boots off and is relaxing in the sun. It's her last day on the trail, her 90 day visa is up. She is looking forward to throwing her boots in the trash as soon as she gets into town.

Soon the hikers that I passed start arriving.

"These are the type of rocks rattlesnakes make their nest around," the first one says as he walks up. The German girl pulls her naked feet closer and scans the area she has been sitting in.

"How far into town?" I ask trying to change the subject.

"6 miles," he says examining the guidebook pages stuffed in a zip lock bag, "but very rocky."

Despite having heard that Pennsylvania was the rocky part of the Appalachian Trail I had secretly hoped that Maryland and West Virginia were as rocky as it got.

It wasn't.

Rocksylvania

The Doyle Hotel is a little farther into town, when I walk in Vickie with her silver and braided pigtails says, "You look too clean cut to be a thru hiker, how can I help you?"

"A room... and a haircut actually."

And a shower the smelly hiker warning sticker on the door reminds me.

I take the time to do a shot of Yukon Jack while she writes up the room receipt. There is a fruit fly dead at the bottom of the shot glass and I realize what kind of hotel stay this is going to be. It's probably sterilized by now I think and do the shot anyway.

Then I'm there three nights.

Much like Trail Days it's a blur.

Neon Mud and Freyr show up and stay the first night. Broken Condom another hiker we had been hiking with on and off since Harpers Ferry stays, without a room he ends up crashing with a couple female south bounders. When they hear that I couldn't get a haircut in town they offer to give me one right there on the second story porch of the Doyle. Why not, whats the worst that could happen.

Only they don't have scissors or clippers so we use the scissors on my Swiss Army knife.

When I wake up in the morning I have a massive hangover and two giant rams horn like spirals carved into the back of my head. They must have felt guilty because they bought me a jar of Nutella.

The Doyle, for all the alcoholic poisoning I inflicted upon myself while staying there, is something special. Part of me envisions living here with the creaking wooden floors and box fans. The bed in my room is missing a wheel and the frame itself is falling apart, the gap in the frame growing larger the longer I stay. The cracked window is held together by thick transparent glue, and I wouldn't have it any other way.

My second zero drags.

I should be hiking.

After tossing and turning the final night, sweating out the last of the alcohol in my system, I could no longer sleep and hit the trail at 6 am. Over budget and self abused.

Whatever toxins haven't been sweated out of my body seep from my pores on the climb out of town. I only have to do 12 miles to the first shelter, take it easy I'm thinking. But when I get there in the early afternoon I feel like a loser. Maybe it's the mosquitoes, maybe it's all the new people coming on the trail from graduating college.

I pop an ibuprofen and some Reeses Pieces for lunch and start running.

"Hey you're Daypack right?" The fresh looking hiker said when I approached him at the spring.

"Cleanshave actually."

"We were thinking about camping here next to the spring, are you planning on staying?"

"Nope, going to try and make another 10 or 15 miles," I say, noticing that he doesn't have a pack with him.

"Good," he says and runs off back down the trail.

The problem is that I now realize where I know him from, and the fact that he is hiking with two other guys doesn't do anything to comfort me. They were just starting the trail from the Doyle and seemed nice enough when I met them. They had never been hiking before and all of their gear was crisp and new. At one point one of them got up and left the bar leaving the rest of his half eaten sandwich behind on the plate.

I didn't want it to go to waste, besides which I was so damn hungry.

So I picked it up and proceeded to finish it.

"There's a fine line between hiker and hobo," Neon Mud had said, "and you my friend just crossed it."

Only the hiker wasn't gone. He soon returned to finish his sandwich after what turned out to be a smoke break. The bar, crowded, his plate almost empty, he looked around for a minute before taking the plate with him back to a table of other hikers.

Did he notice that I ate most of his sandwich?

Was he waiting down the trail with his friends for a little revenge?

Ah, fuck.

Sure enough they were waiting for me not much further down the trail. They had their packs off and were standing on both sides of the trail that was blocked by a large fallen tree. One in the middle, one hiker on either side.

I consider giving them the last $10 in my pocket by way of apology for eating the sandwich only to think that I have already spent enough money and there had to be another outcome. Besides which they left two days ahead of me meaning they have only averaged 9 miles per day.

They don't have their trail legs yet.

So I smile.

Keep the conversation friendly, polite and light. Any edge of tension seems to seep out of them as I flank them and make my way over the fallen tree before they know what I'm doing.

They are tired and from the looks of it won't make it much longer out here on the trail.

"Hey guys," I say getting ready to cruise down the trail, "get some rest, relax and enjoy yourself. Remember there is no hurry. Just have fun, and good luck."

I see them look at each other as I turn away. Fun? They in no way think any of this is fun.

But do I think it's fun I wonder as I somehow find renewed energy to run up the side of Stony Mountain from Clark's Valley.

I don't know about fun. Maybe invincible. It makes me feel invincible at times. Until the blisters slow me down and everything starts aching and I limp into Rausch Gap Shelter to a shocked Neon Mud, Freyr and Broken Condom.

"How the hell did you catch up with us?"

I can't remember how I got to the airport in Tennessee.

The customer service agent is saying I can't board the flight, my file has been flagged.

"Flagged? By who?" I ask.

"Baltimore Jack," she says matter of factly.

It seems that Baltimore Jack has put something down in my permanent Appalachian Trail Record and the CSA cannot allow me to finish.

"I'm sorry," she says, "but he's the son of the owner of the Appalachian Trail. There's nothing I can do."

She is expecting a fight or an argument because of what's in my file.

"I understand," I tell her, "It's not your fault."

I'll just have to figure out how to do the trail another way.

Then, walking away, I start to get upset at the absurdity of not being able to finish the trail because of some stupid mark in my file that I'm not even allowed to see. I go back to the counter, frustrated and angry and get ready to have it out with her, to demand that some other travel option has to be found, when I wake up.

In my sleeping bag at the Rausch Gap Shelter.

And I realize that the sign in my dream that said Tennessee Airport had letters randomly capitalized.

TEnNesSeE.

I'm so frustrated I want to hit something.

All morning the hike out of town is like that, negative counter productive thoughts running through my head. No matter how fast I hike it feels like I'm not gaining any ground.

Then the I-81 underpass, the climb up is rocky and it may as well have rained since I'm drenched in sweat. It drips freely from my eyebrows, shirt and shorts.

112

Everywhere the trail is strewn with rocks covered in poison ivy and the bugs seemed to have returned with a vengeance. Mosquitoes try to land and bite my wrists, hands and arms. They swarm around my eyes and every exhale is directed up out of my mouth in an attempt to drive them away.

There is too much noise in my head and the constant assault of the mosquitoes is pushing me over the edge.

I want to scream.

Instead I give up. I drop my pack in what turns out to be a patch of poison ivy. I force myself to exhale some of the tension without screaming and move my backpack to a clearer spot on the ground.

"Try to cool down, drink some water" I tell myself.

There is a cell phone signal and I'm happy for the distraction.

I eat half a jar of Nutella and clear out my voice mail by the time I've relaxed enough to continue hiking.

After that I push myself harder, faster. It's all rock fields and foot pain. Shin splints and I'm limping again the last 4 miles into 501 Shelter. I'm stumbling and sweating.

Where is this place?

The shelter is renowned for the ability to have pizza delivered and sure enough a section hiker does a little trail magic and buys a couple large pizzas for the thru hikers. Despite everyone being hungry beyond belief they all make sure everyone has had a slice before going for their second, and when there is only a couple of slices left everyone gets asked if they have had enough.

Then, just after dark, a family of Mennonites shows up with gallons of ice cream for the hikers. It's their fathers birthday and want he wanted was to do trail magic for hikers. Him and his sons had hiked big sections in 2008, the wet year that saw the highest drop out rate ever. So of course the first thing he asks about is the weather.

None of us have had any problems with the rain and this changes the fathers expression to one of slight sadness. Like a lost opportunity. He just chose the wrong year to hike.

The trail out of 501 Shelter is rocky. The going is slow and time drags. I trip and fall and hate northern Pennsylvania. I also didn't pack out water and my underwear is chaffing.

I want to punch babies.

I want to be alone, let everyone get ahead of me, I feel like I need a zero to recuperate from my zero's.

I start thinking about the rage again. The primal urge for aggression, triggered by the primal urge for sex. Those beautiful naked girls, my extreme, uncontrollable hate. Both of those are a part of me, for good or bad, and suppression or avoidance of that urge could cause itself to manifest in other ways.

Less healthy ways.

I need to find a proper balance. That this rage is just a glimpse of what I have bottled up inside bothers me less than the fact that I have no experience in how to handle it.

If Pennsylvania is going to redeem itself then the Pinnacle is it. At 1,635 feet it has an awesome view of the surrounding farmland and is said to be the best on the AT in Pennsylvania. Eagles and turkey vultures circle above and below the view.

Lunch is a jar of peanut butter because I forgot water again. Luckily a couple packing up their tent has an extra bottle from the cooler they don't want to carry. I'm about to cry when they dump the rest of their ice into the illegal fire pit.

"At least you don't smell like a hiker," they say.

Eckville Shelter is too nice. I take a cold shower and do some laundry in a bucket and read.

When another thru hiker finally shows up I realize that he has started his hike almost a month after me. I start to think of why I'm so far behind him, I start to try to explain myself, to justify the week in Damascus, the days in Duncannon. And just like that it's gone. That rush, the competition is no longer there. This isn't even about completing the hike anymore.

It's about me, the moment, this day.

I still end up running 24 miles the next day, but it's a leisurely run.

The George W. Outerbridge Shelter is tiny, it sleeps six and doesn't have a privy. What bothered me was the large group of Outward Bound hikers. Between them and the day hikers out for the fourth of July weekend and the rocky terrain I didn't think many people would be tenting. But there was room, and I planned on going into town for resupply the next day.

What really sold it was the open area of trees where a few people said that we might be able to catch a glimpse of the fireworks show.

"Is that music I hear?" The young daughter of a former thru hiker asks.

Sure enough the sound of Patsy Cline climbs up the trail ahead of the beams of two head lamps stumbling in the darkness.

Carrying a small boombox is a guy in his late 50's wearing a wife beater shirt and stumbling, partly because he is drunk, partly because he has one glass eye. He is followed by his 19 year old son who looks like he has never spent a day in the woods never mind been out for a whole night. They are unkempt and price tags hang from their brand new gear.

When he was 9 years old he was in a gang. The gang leader had told him he was to young and to go home. He refused. To scare him the gang leader pulled out a knife which led to him being slashed across the face. His eye fell out of the socket, dangling by the retina.

"Man it was so cool, to be standing there but so dizzy," he says explaining that he could still see out of the exposed eye.

"They didn't have none of this repair surgery they have now, they snipped it it and threw it in a garbage can. Bastards."

He lost his teeth when he was 21, in a gang fight.

In Canada he was arrested for cooking burgers. He was hungry, broke into a school and cooked himself some dinner. Received 6 months in jail where they fed him regularly. The problem was all the prison riots at the time extended his stay.

Came home to the US and ingested 100 hits of acid. Crawled across a four lane highway and was institutionalized for a bit.

His son is awkward and embarrassed about his father telling stories. Keeps mentioning that he needs weed. His father says something about alcohol fetal syndrome and that stupid bitch. A section hiker says maybe you shouldn't say that in front of your son.

"Yeah, she is a stupid fat bitch," the son chimes in.

They had shoplifted everything they brought up with them tonight.

"Even the sparklers," he says holding a case in his hand. He drops the entire box on the fire and everyone scatters. Tom Jones comes on the jukebox and he is belting out "It's not unusual" at the top of his lungs while the sparklers all burn and fizzle.

I'm dying laughing, tears streaming down my face. All the day hikers and children are huddled in the shelter and in their tents petrified. No one is sleeping.

"I came out here to get fucked up!" he says to himself, alone by the fire.

"My son broke my heart," he yells into the shelter where we all pretend to sleep. "He won't go to community college. All he does is sit at home and play Call of Duty."

He goes to change the CD and we tell him that it's late, he shouldn't play any more.

"No more? No one wants me around," he says, "If I had some weed I could sleep."

He quiets down and wanders over to the fire. There is a loud thump and a few of us jump up expecting him to have fallen into the fire, only he is slamming large rocks into the ground. Testing them to be used as a pillow.

He lumbers into the shelter dropping a huge rock on the wooden floor and prepares to sleep next to me. When he pulls off his pants I thank god that he is at least wearing underwear.

"Oh, I almost forgot," he says and pulls a 6 inch blade out of it's sheath and lays it next to him.

"In case someone wants to rob me on their appointment..." he says, the thought fading.

Chances are slim that this guy is going to murder anyone, still the thought of this guy, drunk, with access to a solid looking hunting knife doesn't make me feel any better. When he starts talking in his sleep I'm a little more anxious. They are all arguments with other people. When I roll over I see that his wallet has fallen out of his pants and is now laying on my sleeping bag.

Are you kidding me?

I move the wallet closer to his sleeping area and he shifts and grabs the knife. He looks around, searching and raises his arm. I'm against the wall ready for anything. He sinks the knife point first into the floor of the shelter just above his head.

"It can stay there," he says and quickly goes back to sleep.

Fuck this. I should just pack and go. Except there is no where to go, it has started pouring rain outside. So I sit there in the dark, listening to the rain and the sleeping rants of this stranger next to me.

It being fourth of July weekend there are a lot of people on the trail and these kids didn't look like they should be out here. The one in the worst shape was complaining the loudest. He said he was a Boy Scout. They smoked cigarettes like they were about to be caught doing something they shouldn't be doing and couldn't start a fire to save their lives.

How are you a Boy Scout? Where's your tinder? Your fire pyramid? What do they teach Boy Scouts these days I wonder?

Then there was the spider problem.

The Boy Scout was afraid of spiders and when one was spotted hanging off the front of the shelter ceiling he became petrified.

"I'll give you all the money in my wallet if you kill that thing," he says to his friends.

They laugh and make fun of him but he is serious.

"Please..." he whines.

I'm disgusted when one of them finally does it for the $7 in his wallet.

"Can we make that for all the spiders the rest of the night?" he asks, desperate.

"No, you said just that spider," his friend says, then turning to the other two, "I'll own his debit card by morning."

I'm thankful when real hikers start to show up and borrow Neon Muds stainless steel cup to cook my first hot meal of the trail. A former hiker named Mechanical Man has a house a mile off the trail and he makes sturdy little alcohol stoves out of soda cans for hikers.

I'm excited about being able to boil water.

Neon Mud and I have a fire going in no time and sit back to relax. The sky is clear and there are an infinite number of stars.

The stars are still there even after you go to bed.

It was a strange thought, of course they're still there.

I listen to the others snoring, alone, I stare up into the endless black of space broken only by tiny dots of flickering light. A galaxy of possibilities.

About 2 am a whimpering sort of sound starts coming out of the shelter. The Boy Scout has a sort of pain in his abdomen. He calls his mom on his cell phone and she tells him that maybe he has to go to the bathroom. So he wakes everybody up to help him find the toilet paper.

"Taylor come with me," he says to his friend after shining the flashlight out into the dark.

"I went earlier, just follow the trail," his friend says from inside his sleeping bag.

"C'mon guys, someone has to go with me."

"Just follow the sign, it says P. ivy or something," another friend chimes in.

The Boy Scout leaves, making it all of 15 feet out into the darkness by himself. He returns to plead for help, he is desperate.

"I'm going to shit my pants," he whines.

When he leaves again I can smell it already, he couldn't wait.

"Taylor it's your fault I had to shit in the middle of the trail," he says when he gets back to the shelter. Knowing how far away the privy was there is no way he made it all the way.

He crawls back into his sleeping bag, the shelter now smelling like human feces, until the silence is broken by the Boy Scouts voice.

"Oh fuck," he says, as if he just noticed there was something extra in his sleeping bag.

Deli to Deli

The climb out of Delaware Water Gap was far easier than people had made it out to be. Then again maybe it was the zero at Church of the Mountain Hostel and all that food I had consumed. The climb was gradual and I was packed full of caffeine, reaching Catfish Fire Tower in no time I realized that I had missed my first New Jersey deli opportunity at the outdoor center.

More miles, faster, I push over rocks like they had in Pennsylvania. But this is New Jersey, the rocks won't be around much longer.

I'm almost at a dead run across open rocky areas and look back to see what looks like a tall dark cloud above DWG dumping thick sheets of rain. I can hear the thunder and decide to keep moving, stay ahead of it.

I'm hustling past groups of Boy Scouts and school groups out backpacking with matching packs.

"You're our 101st friend," a cheery school girl says as I pass. They are taking a break off to the side of the trail, she asks how far I'm going.

"Maine," I say simply wanting to keep up the momentum, thinking about the steak house 10 or so miles away.

"Good luck with that," she replies with obvious disbelief, but I'm already gone.

Moving so fast I don't even notice when I pass the turn off for Brink Shelter. I'm dying of thirst and hauling ass. My upper body is covered in sweat and smashed bugs. Spots of blood are smeared here and there where a mosquito managed to get a taste before being crushed against my dirty sweaty skin. The bugs add to the urgency of the hike.

Then the smell starts and I can hear the road down at Culvers Gap.

The smell of steak.

There is no other option, I must eat.

Their packs were stacked outside, leaning against the porch. Neon Mud and friends, Freyr, Broken Condom all had left a day before and here I was, seven hours of hiking and I had caught up with them. Fucking caffeine, I couldn't stop vibrating. My whole body felt electric.

"Cleanshave!" The chorus erupts when I walk in, wired and dehydrated. Drinking my third water I notice the tick dug into my calf. Pinch him and pull him out but he is dug in good. I'm worried that I squeezed him wrong, that I didn't pinch him up high enough and that if it's body gets squeezed they can vomit back into your blood stream.

I've already passed two thru hikers who had come down with Lyme Disease.

Only now that I was there I was no longer hungry. Everyone else had been there for a few hours and are getting ready to leave. Satisfy my weird craving for French Onion Soup and pack out a steak and cheese sub.

I'm the first one to the trail and easily cruising at four miles per hour. I can feel the food in my stomach, pushing out and aching. But I'm still wired. The cool down and calories were all I needed. I did 31.4 miles and I'm thinking about pushing on to the next shelter. The only thing that stops me is the thought of the steak and cheese sub in my backpack with extra mayonnaise. The thought of it sitting for another couple hours in my hot backpack.

Time to eat again.

In the morning we all stagger out of the shelter at different times. Some early, some later.

Some hikers stop to pick blueberries along the trail but I keep hiking. I like the new faster pace. Besides which the heat of the day makes the blueberries warm, they need to be chilled.

Then someones dog is running alongside the trail and it is weird because I haven't seen any other hikers in a while and we are pretty far out for a casual stroll with your pet. When the second animal starts moving away from me I realize that they aren't dogs. They are bear cubs heading to a nearby tree for safety.

I immediately stop and look for the mother bear.

She is 25 feet away standing on her hind legs staring at me.

I'm thinking about the camera shot. She is kind of far away to get a good picture with my cell phone, and it's a little on the dark side too with the foliage...

And then I realize that she is still staring at me, from only 25 feet away. I'm not exactly between her and her cubs but I'm a hell of a lot closer to them than she is, and she could probably cover that 25 feet in a heartbeat if she wanted too.

Act casual I think to myself, and then without realizing how stupid it seems I pretend to check the time on my nonexistent wrist watch. The international sign for nonchalant.

I turn my body away from her and the cubs without turning my back towards them and casually walk away as I pretend that something else has caught my interest.

I have to catch myself from starting to whistle as I slowly back down the trail.

She is still watching as I move to a side trail where the foliage and trees will block her view.

And I wait.

Neon Mud had run into his first group of bears not too long ago in the middle of the trail. They refused to move and he realized that they were not afraid of him in the slightest. He backed down the trail and smoked a cigarette to pass the time.

I don't smoke but consider eating a Snickers to kill a little time. The problem is that sitting there has drawn a cloud of mosquitoes, all swarming for my blood. I slap and dance trying to shake them off but there are too many of them, I'll never be able to kill them all.

Bear or no bear, I have to move. I wack my poles together to try and make some noise, to let the mother bear know where I am. There is movement in the brush near where I had seen her last, the cubs are no longer in the trees. Hopefully they are moving deeper into the woods and not farther up the trail.

Then one of the cubs shimmeys up a lone tree off to the side of the trail.

I'm not between them, damn close but not between I think continuing to wack my poles together. Luckily the trail veers to the right and the cub is in a tree off to the left. Looking back to see if anything is following I almost kill myself tripping on rocks.

Focus on the trail, put some distance between us.

For some reason my heart isn't beating any faster than normal and I'm not really worried about the bear. My first inclination upon seeing the bear had been to wave, but putting a little space between us now seemed to be prudent.

Something I'll never understand is hikers with large knives. Personally I see it as a sign that there is something off about you mentally and it is just one of the indicators that you are not a "real" hiker, that you are in fact a hobo.

It was at Rutherford Shelter where I met Witchy. I'd like to say that he met me as well but from the size of his pupils and the way he swayed back and forth I wasn't sure if he knew I was real. He was wearing jeans and had a large knife strapped to his leg.

"How much farther is High Point?" he asks, "I'm hoping to go into town to resupply."

"I could use a food resupply myself," I say hoping that will discourage him from asking me for any handouts.

He looks around, back to the shelter where he has several different colored cotton bandanas hanging up to dry. He sways a little turning back in my direction, never looking at me, but through me.

"I need gear," he says and I notice that there is no backpack, no tent, no sleeping bag. All he has is the jeans he is wearing and the knife.

The big knife that takes up most of the length of his thigh.

The only thing that stops me from walking away is that I'm pretty sure that whatever dimension he is operating in is not the same one that I currently inhabit. That and the fact that it looks like he is still standing due to nothing more than luck.

He must have sensed my hesitation because he starts to tell me about how all of his stuff had been stolen. He had left it there in the shelter and when he came back it was gone. "The rangers at park headquarters are only a few miles away," I tell him.

"If they came across your gear in the shelter they may have thought it was abandoned property. You should go on up and see if they are holding any of your stuff."

Conflict rolls across his face and his eyes search the area. Maybe his eyes are looking back inside his head at memories. Incidents with park rangers, his stuff and how he needs to get his gear back. Maybe he is too well known to the rangers for him to hope to get his stuff back. He is still standing there like that when I say goodbye. There is no response, maybe later he will realize that I have left, maybe he'll wonder if I was ever really there.

Not much farther on I pass a south bounder, and the first thing I notice, besides his 100 pound pack is the large bowie knife strapped to his leg.

"I hate hiking in the rain," he says angrily. I look up through the canopy of trees, it's not really a rain, more like a mist, but there was something about the way he said it, like he was trying to suck me into a conversation. I notice his prison tattoos as he starts to take off his pack.

"That's a pretty good size pack," I say, slowing my stride but not really stopping. If he gets the pack off he will be too agile, too fast, and there is nothing friendly about him.

"Don't like hiking in the rain," he grunts having a hard time maneuvering the heavy pack. I want to ask him if he knows how far I am from the secret shelter, only I don't want to tip him off if he doesn't already know about it. Besides which I don't want him knowing where I'll be sleeping.

"Hopefully the rain will hold off until you can get to the shelter. Have a good hike."

He is still talking to himself as I make my way over the next hill.

The sprinkling rain picked up a little more and kept threatening to turn into a downpour. Thunder rumbled through the sky but the canopy of trees had kept me dry. Even when the trail cut through fields it usually followed the edge with it's overhang of branches.

It was all so beautiful and amazing. A perfect day to hike, cool and quiet, and yet I was a little sad. I was sure that I must have missed the turn off to the secret shelter. That it was hidden somehow and I didn't have the correct information. I stopped to consult my companion again. Three road crossings and I should have been there, but here I was and there was no trail, no obvious sign.

Maybe a little farther.

The secret shelter is all that anyone on the trail has been talking about for the last two days. It was all rumors and at first they teased me about it. I was just a day hiker with my little day pack. They teased Broken Condom that he was just a section hiker and couldn't stay there either.

"Don't let them get you down Broken Condom. You're a LASER. Long Ass Section Hiker."

The secret shelter was an unofficial shelter that was built and maintained on someones private property not too far off the trail. By the time I cross my fifth road I convince myself that it was somewhere around the fourth road crossing a mile or so back. No sense in turning around though, the next shelter is only five or so miles away and it looks like a storm is moving up from behind me.

Resolved to push on I pick up my pace.

Then I see the sign. By the time the rain turns into a heavy downpour I am safely inside the secret shelter. There are no bunks and no electricity but the grassy fields that surround it are amazing. Broken Condom is the only hiker to show up that I expected. A few others straggle in, change and try to dry out. I sit out on the covered front porch until midnight listening to the rain, watching the intermittent firefly's.

I'm awake by 6am. Packed and snacked.

The hike around Wallkill and through the swamps is some of the best hiking yet on the trail. Without the mosquitoes New Jersey would easily be the best state on the Appalachian

Trail. Deer and turkeys roam around an abandoned house where I refill my water bottle. I keep passing section hikers, day hikers and flip floppers all day long. The hiking is so easy I feel like I'm floating. The day is neither too hot nor too humid, there isn't a cloud in the sky.

Across Pochuck Footbridge I slow down and take my time. I know there is a place up ahead to get ice cream just off the trail. I opt for a butter pecan milkshake and take my shoes and socks off to dry. For the first time I'm starting to think that my shoes won't make it all the way to Katahdin. The duct tape that I had hoped would hold them together hadn't even lasted the whole day coming out of DWG.

Another thru hiker joins me, he hadn't known about the place but decided to make a stop after I had mentioned where I was going. I want to sit here forever, eat ice cream and savor this feeling. More hikers show up though and they all claim to be heading to the same shelter for the night. Wawayanda, where I planned on staying, holds 6 people. A quick head count and it looks like seven people here, not including myself, are headed there for the night.

Across the road the trail continues up, 1,000 feet straight up Wawayanda Mountain. The view is incredible and in the cool breeze I wonder what all this easy hiking has done to my trail legs.

The wind is strong and cool. Energizing and refreshing. I sit for a while and the peaceful feeling washes over me again. In the distance I can see the monument I walked past the day before. Below me I can see colorful little backpacks making their way up the trail to the base of the mountain where they disappear into the trees.

I pack up and walk, slow, to a stream crossing where I dunk my head, wash off some of the salt sticking to my body and trekking poles. Further up and the breeze starts again, clean and fresh, like I'm being baptized by nature. All my sins washed away.

Then I'm at the shelter and the mosquitoes start to swarm. I swat them away and realize that I'm back in New Jersey.

At least it's not Pennsylvania.

I had just finished going to the bathroom when I turned around to the shock of seeing what had just come out of me resting on the back rim of the toilet seat. It wasn't any kind of normal poop, it was huge. About the size of my forearm and looked to be composed of meat and bloody mucus.

Like a tumor.

"That came out of me?" I wondered as I unrolled some toilet paper to try and push it into the toilet. But when I turned back it was gone.

Then I was in a driveway somewhere and an old friend is suggesting that we hike the AT.

It sounds like a great idea and ask if he grabbed my gear as we are heading out. Sure enough he grabbed my backpack, only when he hands it over I have this overwhelming need to check it's contents.

It is almost empty. There is maybe a small flashlight and a sleeping bag.

A nervous feeling creeps over me about all the other things I'll need for the trail. Then and idea occurs, how cool would it be to hike with minimal gear? How much easier would the trail be? Light and free.

Easy hiking.

The sound of people banging around makes me realize that I have already hiked the AT.

More noise from the southbound section hikers who have decided to cook breakfast inside the shelter instead of out on the picnic table brings me completely out of the dream.

I'm still hiking the AT.

I try to fall back asleep after they have finished packing only to have that desire crushed by the cigarette smoke drifting into my face. They are smoking at the entrance of the shelter with the smoke clearly drifting straight in, no concern whatsoever for the rest of us sleeping.

Fucking section hikers.

The idea was 27 miles to Fingerboard Shelter, pushing big miles to resupply. But something about the dream keeps pulling at the edge of my consciousness. How gross it was at the beginning, how the idea of having less in my pack made me feel like I could do anything.

I spend an inordinate amount of time shaving and brushing my teeth in the bathroom of the park office and realize that I'm not really going anywhere today. Maybe the creamery on 17A, maybe lunch.

The rest will take care of itself.

Hike to the New Jersey/New York state line, to Prospect Rock for the view.

Then, suddenly, I'm face to face with another bear.

There is absolutely no reaction on my part, no skipped heart beat, no fast breathing or panicked reaction.

It's a bear.

And it is not moving, just staring back at me standing there on it's hind legs while it's cubs run further into the woods. I nod my head as if to ask if she was going to follow them but she doesn't move. I backtrack a few feet until I am out of her view and sit on a rock.

Maybe I should have gone further away before I pulled off my backpack and mixed a lemon lime sports drink. Maybe...

The sound of heavy footsteps, breaking branches and large heavy feet moving through the underbrush snaps me back to full attention. I breathe a sigh of relief as it becomes apparent that they are moving off, deeper into the woods and away from the trail.

The shade is nice and the rock comfortable. Give the bears some time to move away and finish the sports drink while it is still cool. Besides, sitting here let's me think about the dream. How different it was from the dreams at the beginning of the hike that were full of clutter. How in the dream I wasn't entirely ready to accept the lack of gear in my pack but was getting used to the idea.

About how whatever that was in the bathroom had come from me.

And it was something that I no longer needed.

The hot dog stand on 17A is cash only, that was expected. The road walk to the creamery finds that it is cash only as well, which is disappointing since I have $1.83. The maddening part is that they do not have an ATM.

The old guy in the hot dog trailer I can understand not taking credit cards, but here, in this air conditioned, permanent building? Seriously, any kid with an iPhone can accept credit cards these days.

Cash is so 1980.

So I backtrack and buy a hot dog for $1.75 and dream about a cold soda to wash it down.

Another thru hiker had hitched into Greenwood Lake and was packing his resupply at one of the tables in front of the hot dog guys trailer. This didn't make the guy any happier to see me and my sweaty money.

"You guys have to move along now, you've been here too long." He tells us from the window after the regular car-driving tourists have left.

Town, resupply. It all sounds so good, so tempting. But hitchhiking is illegal in New York.

I stand by the roadside and try to look pathetic, try to give every indication that I need a ride short of sticking out my thumb. And then I start walking, the thought of food compels me down the road, and it is all downhill into town.

If I had known it was going to come to this I would have hiked the blue blaze from the trail into town instead of walking down the hot, dangerous road.

The ATM at the convenience store is out of service.

The Indian lady at Subway swipes the card so hard I think she is going to break it. She can't make it work, "It's no good. Do you have another way to pay?"

"NO!" I want to scream, "Just let me eat!"

Luckily the pharmacy next door gives cash back and the card actually goes through.

Despite my better judgment I return to Subway where the owner skimps on every topping.

Condiments? Mayonnaise, yellow mustard, oil, vinegar.

"Wait! Stop!" I yell as she squeezes brown mustard all over the sandwich.

"Yellow mustard!" I say getting frustrated, the sandwich so close, "What don't you understand about yellow mustard?"

"Mustard," she says holding up the bottle.

"No," I say, "Yellow mustard."

She doesn't understand and I'm feeling petty, I'm ready to walk out, tell her to go fuck herself and find some real food. But I'm so fucking hungry and the sandwich is right behind the glass and there isn't a container of yellow mustard in sight.

"No French Mustard. Just wipe it all off."

She looks at me like I'm crazy. Maybe I am. I just want my sandwich a certain way that I had in my head since I saw the Subway sign. Before she abused my card and made me leave to get cash.

There's air conditioning here, I try to reassure myself, free soda refills and a bathroom.

Calm down.

Two hours later I'm full and back out in the sun walking the 2 miles uphill, out of town and back to the trail. The views from Cat Rocks and Eastern Pinnacles are hard to enjoy with the sharp stomach pains and bloated gassiness from the sandwich, but I love the breeze.

There are lots of town people out on the trail with only a bottle of water, their car not too far away. It is more than a little annoying and I'm having a hard time holding on to the peacefulness that a full stomach can bring.

Despite the gas pains.

Wildcat Shelter is closer than I'd wanted, less than .3 miles from Cat Rocks and all those tourists. There is a bear box that looks like someones rusted toolbox from the back of their pickup truck and all the other hikers are tenting so I have the shelter all to myself. All to myself that is except the birds nest in the back with the chirping baby birds.

I hope they sleep at night.

Another thru hiker I had never seen before, though I suspect he is a section hiker, cooks his dinner on the fire I built in front of the shelter. I'm happy for the company but all he wants to talk about is terrorists on the trail. He is an ex cop, and obsessed with terrorism.

"The things I know about how to take down the trail," he says, "I shouldn't say any more."

I wish you wouldn't I'm thinking as he continues along another tangent.

Another hiker gathered around the fire moves off to make a cell phone call. I can't help but over hear his half of the conversation, "It's happening again. Can you pick me up?"

I look up to the sky, through the trees, expecting an extraction team anytime. Helicopters, men in black, ninjas. All descending from ropes dropped at the last minute.

Later I learn that he has an old stress fracture and it is acting up again.

The sun sets and the hikers who had gathered around the fire in front of the shelter wander off to their tents and hammocks for the night leaving me alone to watch ants escape from the inside of a log in the fire. They test where the heat is greatest, looking for a way out, their home on fire. Some carrying eggs, frantically running around, trying the same directions over and over.

I imagine what it must be like, inside the log. Smoke and steam.

Confusion.

Incredible heat being channeled through whatever tunnels they have built.

Do ants feel fear?

I roll the log so part of it is outside the fire ring. I don't know if any of them make it but at least now they have a chance. A way to go that won't sear their limbs off their bodies from the intense heat.

I don't look at the log anymore. That is their opportunity, use it or lose it.

Sleep is impossible, not because of the ants and their home on fire but because of the buzz of mosquitoes. Wrapped in my silk cocoon from head to toe with my sweatshirt pulled up over my head they sting or bite, whatever it is that they do. I swat them away hoping to kill enough of them that I can make a dent in their population.

It doesn't seem to be working.

To pass the time and direct my anger I try to devise non electrical devices for installation in the shelters that would kill off the surrounding mosquito horde. I would kill every single one of them if I had the opportunity.

Mosquito genocide.

They pierce through the silk cover, sometimes staining it red with blood when I manage to smash one, ruining my train of thought.

It's too much.

The sound of buzzing, the itch.

I want to scream, the sun can't come up early enough.

I pack my bag while slapping at my head, arms and legs. No sleep, I'm tired and yet I'm on the trail with the earliest start ever. Breakfast, I'm hoping for an opening in the trees, a reprieve from the constant swarm of mosquitoes that feed off of me, a clear ridge with a view of the rising sun.

I'm frantic, trying to move fast and stay ahead of the cloud, slapping at the black flies on the back of my head, in my hair. Watching for mosquitoes landing on my arms.

Then I scare a group of bears on the trail.

I had come up so fast that they were startled to see me coming up on them from less than 15 feet away. They reflexively backed away from my presence and off to the side of the trail, enough that I consider running by them, not enough that I actually do.

I slow down and try to make noise with my poles to scare them away but the bug cloud overtakes me and the bears are still way too close, they refuse to move any more. The bug swarm is too much, I can't take it anymore, suddenly the bears seem like less of a threat.

I push past the bears staring at me from the side of the trail and try to keep moving, hoping that they don't follow. That they don't take a swipe at me with their large sharp paws as I pass. I hope that it all happened so fast they'll be wondering if it really ever occurred.

This is madness.

In all of the world I hate only two things, mosquitoes are one of them.

Sure, being mauled to death by bears should be something I'm opposed to as well but right now it isn't even on my list. Luckily they are still standing there watching me walk away and haven't moved from where they were when I passed. But having to turn around to see if I was being pursued, if this was the most stupid thing I had ever done, made my eyes refocus closer, to the thick cloud of bugs steps behind.

Never mind the ones that managed to attach themselves to my skin and drain my blood, that was only a small portion of what I had to deal with if I slowed down in the slightest.

In the haze of frantic activity I realize that all of a sudden I'm hand over hand climbing. Everything else is forgotten as I reach Mombasha High Point, my left knee is a mass of welts from mosquito bites.

No bugs. Sun and a breeze.

I want to nap in the sun on the hard rock.

I don't want to do this anymore, not the bugs.

I'm delirious, sweating and over heated. I haven't been eating right. No Gatorade so my electrolytes are probably low. Caffeine pills for four days straight, maybe I'm a little burnt out. I force myself to get up and walk, not even looking at the trail. I'm thinking about the Tuxedo Motel, air conditioning and cable TV.

Get a room early, take a nap.

Then I'm out of breath wondering how I got down to the road so fast at what used to be the payphone on route 17. The phone itself has been ripped out, the rusting hulk of a stand in front of the Welcome to Harriman State Park sign crushes my hopes.

No payphone, no motel.

"A motel room is too expensive anyway. No matter how tempting it sounds." I tell myself dropping to the ground and leaning on the empty payphone stand for support.

Eating a Snickers I realized that I wanted to quit. I wasn't down, wasn't depressed.

Just done.

"For the day." The voice in my head reminded me.

An hour later I forced myself up. Not a single thought had run through my mind the entire time that I sat there. The only thing that got me moving was a distant voice, "You can sit here until you die or we can keep moving to the vending machines at Tiorati Circle."

It was so quiet and vague, and yet the voice knew exactly what would motivate me to start moving, to keep walking.

Cold Coca-Cola.

Hungry, tired and out of my mind, Tiorati Circle was an oasis.

Families at the beach, children happy and screaming in the water, everyone enjoying themselves, refugees from downtown New York looking for something besides the concrete jungle as a way to spend their weekend.

Was it a weekend? I wasn't sure.

The shower was cold and welcome. I drank a cold Coke while washing my socks in the shower, watching the dark brown dirt that had accumulated run off my clothes and down the drain. Another overpriced can of soda and I'm feeling better.

Three hours of doing nothing. Nothing resolved. Nothing to think about.

Children play in the water fountain I have to drink from, their parents nearby at picnic tables, grilling food.

It all smells so good.

I'm too clean cut, I don't look homeless enough.

No one offers any food and I don't ask.

I suppress my inner Yogi and resist the urge to run away with a picnic basket. The hike out is quiet, the woods are on the cool side of hot and I don't even break a sweat.

By the time I'm climbing Bear Mountain it has to be in the 90's.

I just want a real lunch.

And a day off hiking.

Maybe a week.

I'm still not down, just drained. I wonder if the extra caffeine combined with the heat and lack of electrolytes can be the cause. Since my protein powder base diet has been off I haven't had the nutrition in my diet that maybe I need.

I find myself just shuffling along, when I think I have gone 5 miles it is actually 2. There seems to be more effort with less return. Every uphill is greeted with a groan and reluctant pause at it's base.

I'll skip the caffeine for the next couple of days and see if there is a change.

I cut through the zoo, passing Walt Whitman's statue, and out the other side. I go left instead of cutting right across Bear Mountain Bridge. I'm hoping for food in Fort Montgomery. Follow the circle around until I'm parallel with Bear Mountain Bridge. I remember it is almost a mile into Fort Montgomery and I want to crash right there.

Fall asleep.

I need to get food, I want to eat.

No more Clif Bars.

I force myself to walk, in the sun, drained of all energy.

At the closest convenience store I drink a half gallon of whole milk, eat an 840 calorie Honey Bun and pack out fritos and a couple cokes.

The guide says there is no elevation change, but there are always elevation changes.

Back out across Bear Bridge, where whats his name had to pay a nickel toll, you know the guy who did this earlier. If you read other books about the Appalachian Trail then you should know who I'm talking about, if you don't know then it really doesn't matter.

And I'm really too dehydrated to remember.

So thirsty.

Not paying attention to the outside world. Watching my feet, so thirsty. I'm on autopilot and so thirsty but the water doesn't seem to be cutting it.

I'm not paying attention.

US 9. The heat is incredible. I try to find shade, for my pack, and go into the store hoping to cool off, to make sense of the world.   The deli makes a Bronx Bomber on a roll. Roast beef, pastrami, fried onions and melted Swiss cheese. Add a 2 liter bottle of coke and my mind draws a blank on resupply.

I have no idea what to get or what I have been eating.

Nothing looks right.

Everything in the store is useless to me. Reeses Pieces? Sesame seeds? I'm trying to get everything at once because the strip on my credit card might not last. I have no idea what is still in my food bag. I can't think of anything to buy. What do I need?

I leave anyway, without getting very much.

I'm dizzy and so very tired hiking up to Graymoor.

Why is my heart going so fast?

At Graymoor I beg another hiker for a Gatorade packet to add to my water. Why didn't I buy any back at the convenience store? I knew I needed electrolytes, I had been saying that for days.

Within 15 minutes I feel better, my brain seems to be working again.

There isn't much to Graymoor, a concrete block covered building and a grass field to tent in, but they have an outdoor shower and it feels so good. So good that it almost makes up for the merciless onslaught of mosquitoes in the area.

Thinking back I couldn't remember a time when I had ever been bitten by a mosquito on my face, other than recently that is. The mosquitoes had been out in force, my sweatshirt hood pulled tight around my head I could listen to them on the outside, near my ear. Driving me insane as I tried to sleep.

I wake up with bites on my chin and at my hairline. My forehead is a mass of welts that extends all the way down between my eyes.

My chin is lumpy and itchy.

The lack of sleep and the mosquito bites does not make my mood any better when I start the days hike. First of all with resupply screwed up so much is up in the air. How far can I go? Where should I stop? Do I go into Pawling, NY tomorrow for resupply? It is way off the trail but I could sleep in their park. That would slow me down by another day.

Then there is the place to get burgers at Canopus Lake, why aren't I carrying cash?

Food, it's all I can think about.

Pizza delivery at RPH.

It's all everyone talked about, not just on the trail but online as well, if you stay at RPH Shelter it is so you can get pizza delivered. Only the guidebook gives me no clue as to how getting a pizza delivered is possible. I understand they can't suggest any pizza place in particular but what they could do is tell us the address of the shelter, or even the name of the town it is located in.

There are no menu's in the shelter, no phone numbers or suggestions in the trail register or on the informational cork board above the desk. There is a phone book but without any idea about where I am I don't know who to call or what to ask. I finally break down and call the caretaker. He has to be roused out of bed, it's three in the afternoon but he is a volunteer. He tells me there is a phone book. I ask what town I'm in. I ask what the address is, he says it's right there in front. He has to search around for something with the address on it and read it back to me.

After the call I go outside and look, the numbers are posted but there is no road sign.

It turns out that we must be well outside Hopewell Junction as most pizza places say they won't deliver this far.

"Do you know of anyone who will?" I ask.

"Not from around here," they say.

I finally find a place that will deliver, place my order, only to have them tell me it is cash only, with a $10 minimum. I have $8.

Fuck this shelter.

I'm sunk. No pizza, no soda. My mood crashes. It is getting too late to hike out, I spent the last several hours trying to figure out how to order pizza. Irritability is a sign of dehydration I try to remind myself.

Finally another thru hiker shows up wanting to order a pizza. He'll split a large with me and has cash, I can pay him back tomorrow. I call back the pizza place that took my order before but now they aren't sure if they can deliver that far out. Besides there is over an hour wait they say.

No problem. Just get it here.

I spend the hour and a half waiting for the cold pizza to be delivered by venting to the trail register.

"Why doesn't the shelter have an info sheet covering how to get a pizza delivered? Something simple like an address, a town, menus for some of the places that do deliver. Even if we are in Hopewell Junction why are we so far out that no one wants to deliver? Is there a nearby town that is closer?"

It feels stupid and petty, I only hope the volunteers that maintain this shelter have some kind of idea about the hunger of a thru hiker and the expectations of this shelter.

Yet another thru hiker comes in having looked forward to getting pizza delivered for the last week. He calls the same pizza place back and with the phone to his ear looks down at our quickly disappearing pizza.

They tell him that they don't deliver here.

"But you just did!?" he cries losing all faith in humanity.

Reluctantly they agree to deliver, he orders a small pepperoni and it comes to $24. He has to borrow the cash from the first thru hiker to pay this exorbitant amount because he had planned on using his credit card as well.

Half an hour later they deliver a large pizza.

At least his is still warm.

Then the trail is a mass of blown down trees. Not just here and there but covering every inch of the ground. Tons of them covered the path as far as I could see, waist deep in places and tangled. I got the impression that this was debris from over a decade ago. You would have thought someone would have cleaned it up by now.

Off to the left of the trail there were several buildings half submerged in water. Then my foot slipped and I realize that downed trees were not resting on the ground, they were far above, suspended by wires stretched between telephone poles.

Somehow I knew the building were research facilities that had been underwater for the entire decade, and only now, recently, had they been exposed to view.

Then my foot slipped through the space in a few of the tree limbs and I woke up in the shelter all alone.

Why a decade? What did the buildings mean?

The hiking is easy and having something to think about helps.

In Falls Village the Toymaker Cafe is closed when I arrive and the pizza place is no where to be found.

"The reason is that there isn't one." The owner of Toymaker Cafe explains. "But if you want to tent in the backyard here there are two different places that will deliver."

"Wow, that would be great except I don't have a tent." I tell him and there doesn't seem to be any trees to stretch out my tarp. Besides, I wasn't sure how he'd take me sleeping in just the bivvy.

"I'll just get a couple of sodas and a snack from the liquor store."

"I'll make you a sandwich." He offers, gesturing me into his cafe through the backdoor.

Even though he is closed he makes me a roast beef sandwich on thick slices of fresh wheat bread and toasts it for me. He throws in a soda and a couple of bags of chips and gives me directions to the outdoor shower next to the electric company maintenance building where I can have a picnic.

"You're celebrating with just a sandwich?" My brain asks when I start heading out of town.

"Why not a drink? Makers Mark from the liquor store. Really enjoy yourself."

Only I don't feel like that guy anymore, the guy who drinks everyday, all the time. I had been doing that for far too long.

Then I stopped in my tracks. About ten years too long. For a decade I had stopped living and allowed myself to wallow in self pity and alcoholism. Now, standing there in the middle of some road in Connecticut I could see how I had let it get worse.

How I had refused to admit it even to myself.

There are times when you have to run.

From the Shays' Rebellion Monument to Route 7 is one of them.

The trail drops down into a swampy area and hordes of mosquitoes attach themselves to you, sucking blood out of every exposed piece of skin.

So you run.

And just when you think it is safe you stop for a moment allowing the cloud of mosquitoes to envelope you.

"Don't stop!" A voice in your head screams, "Keep moving!"

So you keep running and the way the air drafts around your arms it is possible for them to attach themselves to your elbows and triceps. So you start slapping at them with the opposite hand, reverse direction reaching across your chest and do it again, all while running. I looked like Carmen Miranda frantically running down the trail doing a little Cha Cha.

And in my head it is a war zone, because these mosquitoes are out for every last piece of me they can get. Land mines explode around me, men scream and cry in the agony of a losing battle. The sound of helicopters roar overhead.

And in the background is a catchy little Cuban jazz tune for me to dance to.

Then you run out onto Route 7 knowing what it is like to be insane.

But at least there is soda available.

The antiques store has a giant Coca Cola bottle sign out from and there is a guy with a beard wearing a brightly colored synthetic shirt.

Hiker.

Him and a friend are trying to hitch into Barrington because there is a huge storm moving in and they warn me against going back out to the trail. I finish the first bottle of soda watching them try to get a ride. The sky is noticeably darker and the wind has picked up. I wander over to the gazebo and charge my phone, not worried about the storm in the least.

I sit and watch the rain for a couple of hours and hike out.

Just off the road and back on the trail the mud is slick and I go down hard, twisting my legs in ways they weren't meant to bend. From my position on the ground I can see the cars going by on the road. Nobody stops, no one even noticed. I roll onto my back and I'm covered in mud, but at least nothing is broken.

I look up at the sky and the rain drops coming straight at me.

If anyone back home could see my huge grin they would think I had lost my mind.

Lyme Disease

I wake up sweating. The headache for the third day in a row pounds my brain against my skull and the kink in my neck muscles doesn't seem to want to work itself out.

I'm falling apart. Everything hurts.

In the bathroom I notice that my left eye is all puffed up to the point of being forced closed. My shoulders and joints hurt to the point that it is hard to move around.

I take an ibuprofen and decide to stay awake. Take a cold shower.

Though I'm riding out the heat wave off trail I'm staying in a house with no air conditioning. There isn't even a fan in the room where I'm sleeping.

My ex-girlfriend picked me up and it was shower, laundry, food.

Teos for hot dogs, it's a local tradition in Pittsfield. Short wieners, meat sauce, onions.

It isn't even noon time and I have consumed well over 2,000 calories already.

We grill steaks back at her parents house and I switch my gear into another, larger backpack she brought from home. That and the sleeping bag, though between the lack of energy and the heat wave I'm thinking about leaving it behind.

"What's this for?" Her niece asks about each item as I try to remember how to pack.

"It's a sleeping bag. I sleep in it to stay warm when I'm outside."

"Do you really sleep in it?"

"Yep."

"Do you really?"

I start drinking a bottle of whiskey looking at all the gear, wondering where it all came from.

Then my nero turns into a nero with a few zeros after that.

I try to sleep in but it isn't working. Take another cold shower to try and cool down. My muscles all hurt and my head feels like it's full of noise.

I dream I'm in the hospital. Three girls visit me, old friends. One of them doesn't feel comfortable sitting on my bed with me and they move out to the visitors area. When I try to follow them out I am awakened by the pain of trying to roll over.

The bones of my hands hurt.

Then it rains and thunders in the morning cooling it off enough that I get a little more sleep. Half awake, half asleep I can't remember a time that it ever took me this long to bounce back. Maybe a day I had thought coming into Massachusetts. Eat some food, cool down and get off the trail, out of this heat wave and I'd be good.

This is something else.

What the hell is wrong with me? Fatigue, joint pain, stiff muscles, headache.

Oh shit.

Lyme Disease.

And for the last three days I had been looking at the circular rash on my calf wondering what the hell it was from. Could it be that tick coming out of Deleware Water Gap?

And this is the worst possible time to figure it out. My ex-girlfriend has to get back to work, I can't stay here any longer. $95 dollars later the doctor at the walk in clinic prescribes doxycycline, 2 pills a day for 21 days.

I'm dropped off back on the trail in Dalton but I'm in no shape to be hiking. I make it as far as the Birdcage, and consider it to be a life saving grace.

Two other hikers there have also just been diagnosed with Lyme Disease. They each got two pills that they are supposed to take at the same time. Since sunburn is a side effect of doxy they plan on night hiking out.

I take the pill and sit on the grass outside the Birdcage in a daze. All around my eyes hurts like I had been punched. A hiker tries to make conversation but I'm not feeling to well, when I tell him my name he knows who I am but we haven't ever met.

"Oh yeah, I've heard of you," he says not wanting to tell the story. I'm thinking it has something to do with the day pack jokes.

"I heard you look like you're 20 but are really 50."

"Yep, pretty much," I say too exhausted to even laugh, sitting in the shade of the maple tree with the weight of the world around my eyes.

Where is my hospital gown and 8 piece puzzle?

"You got sick," the voice inside my head says, "that's not supposed to happen."

"You're weak."

I stare off into the distance, at nothing in particular. Lay down in the grass. Sit up. I want to bend the rest of this trail over and fuck it. Then I lose my train of thought.

I should be angry at something I vaguely remember.

I want the sunburn. I want every piece of flesh burned off of my body. My sacrifice, to hike with black charred flakes of charcoal skin falling from my arms and face revealing the white dry ancient skeleton underneath. My jaw falling from the rest of my skull, my bones falling in a pile at the base of the Katahdin sign.

I want the headaches to stop.

The second dose of doxy was worse than the first. I was stuck in the shuttle for resupply and had no where to vomit. And I was damn sure I was going to vomit. The pill didn't want to stay down, my mouth filling with saliva. When I kept swallowing a few nearby hikers made some room and asked if everything was OK.

"I think I'm going to be sick."

"Just a little further," they said backing away, looking for anything that I could puke into. Another hiker who looks like he is going to puke just from watching me hands me a dirty towel.

144

Just focus on breathing.

Neon Mud, Freyr and Broken Condom are all taking a beer-o, a zero to drink beer, and I sleep through another day. Rob, the owner of the Birdcage, wants to make sure I'm OK to hike out in the morning. I pop another doxy and tell him I'll take it slow. The truth is I plan on crushing out some miles, only the new pack seems way too heavy and bulky.

The mosquitoes are awful and by the time I make it the 4 miles to Gore Pond my knees hurt and I feel tired and depressed. I did this to myself, I thought I was above Lymes Disease. That doesn't happen to me. Why didn't I just start eating cloves of garlic like I had planned? Maybe that would have helped.

What can I do now except hike?

I smile up at the sky, the cloud cover is a blessing that will keep me from getting too sunburned. I start to sweat and it feels like my brain is starting to function again.

How long has it been?

The rain is cool and cold front moves in causing me to shiver. The hairs on my arm are standing out straight and I feel it again. A cold baptism, I am born again from diseased dead corpse. Everything washed away, clean.

The rain continues, harder, I'm soaked and cold, my hands white and puckered. I'm starting to lose feeling in the tips of my fingers.

This is the best day ever!

Forget the rain jacket. The rain slows to a dense fog, thunder rolls away in the distance and the wind howls through the trees dropping ice cold water droplets on me. Each and every drop exquisite, every color, every sound fantastic.

Beautiful.

I pass Broken Condom on the way to the summit of Mount Greylock. He has his rain jacket on and is freezing. I'm still in my t-shirt and smiling like a madman.

Up ahead through the fog I can hear Freyr doing his sheep call. We all made it to the emergency shelter on top of

Greylock, and there is a fire going with plenty of firewood outside.

"There's a huge storm rolling in right?"

It doesn't matter who said it, we all wanted to stay.

The ranger shows up at 8pm.

"I'm not going to kick you guys out tonight," he says. "But I don't want you telling other hikers it is OK to camp here." His arms are folded, he is very serious.

"We have problems with you guys pooping all over the summit."

I'm just excited to be on top of the mountain in a huge thunder and lightning storm.

The robot walks towards me with an awkward gait. It is orange and has a thick chest and stiff legs and arms. It topples over under it's own weight and the top splits open spilling pictures all over the ground. The seam is ripped on the top, near the brain I think, and realize that it is not a robot, it is my backpack.

The top part of a backpack is called a brain.

The pictures are memories.

Nero the North

Vermud.

As soon as I crossed the state line into Vermont it had started raining.

The trail is packed with 17 – 18 year old kids out with some Ukrainian group. They don't seem to have any supervisors because when I get into Congdon Shelter the kids are carving their names into the shelters walls.

Freyr, Neon Mud and Broken Condom all arrive at the shelter and decide to stay for the night as well.

One of the Ukrainian Club students has two propane tanks in his hand and he is trying to figure out how to get the propane out of one into the other. He is trying to unscrew the top.

"Sometimes you have to use a hammer," I say, "they can get stuck real tight."

"Really?" he asks looking for something heavy.

We all just laugh.

"Can you help me with my zipper?" Broken Condom asks, noting the pliers the kid grabbed to try and unscrew the lid to the propane tank and we all burst out laughing again.

"What? You never used that pickup line?" Broken Condom asks innocently.

After that we all seem to be taking it slower.

People are already talking about what they are going to do when this is done. Finding work on oil rigs or fishing boats, something outdoors. Nobody knows what's waiting for them back home. Some of them don't want to think about it and more than a few have slowed way down.

One thru hiker that has kept pace is now only hiking 11 miles a day.

I pass Neon Mud on the trail taking a long smoke break, he is calling in reservations to Green Mountain Hostel. We already killed a day in Bennington at the Vortex but what the hell. I had been hiking in such a pleasant mood that I had failed to realize that I was almost out of food.

"Nero the North," Neon Mud says.

"What do you figure? Four months to do 80% of the trail, two or three months to do the last 20%?"

"Sounds about right," he says laying back in the pine needles next to Stratton Pond.

The drizzle is amazing, 8 miles go by in the blink of an eye and I'm standing at the edge of Prospect Rock. The edge disappears into white, blank clouds that swirl around me and in the distance. A momentary peek at the treeline and it disappears.

Cross the road and back into the magic of the woods.

The wet weather really has a noticeable effect on my alcohol stove. Sometimes it will take a few attempts to boil water. Only it never seems to bother me, neither does being cold and wet.

All of a sudden I'm watching the rain from Spruce Peak Shelter and I think about sitting here 40 years from now. Will I still think back fondly on this hike or will I consider it to have been too hard? Will I appreciate being inside this shelter then as much as I do now, even without a light or heat?

I'm suddenly filled with an appreciation for the moment.

A fleeting glimpse of something perfect.

I had heard about some hikers slowing down towards the end of the hike, doing shorter mile days to stretch out the amount of time they were out here.

Putting off the end for as long as possible.

After all, what was there to go home too?

And then work calls while I'm staying at the Inn at the Long Trail where despite having only $200 left to finish the trail Neon Mud, Freyr and I split a room.

My sister failed to show up for her shift in the restaurant. I had helped her get the job bussing tables because she needed the money and had been out of work for a long time. At first it was just a few shifts here and there, only that was supposed to to turn into a regular thing.

Now she was a no call, no show.

I call my mom but there is no answer, their phone is out of service.

Why can't they keep it together? Why do I need to worry about making sure they follow through and keep a job?

Why do I let this shit affect me?

The truth is I have felt so damn good lately. Everything is awesome.

But this thing with my family was something else, a trigger into something deeper.

Getting a hitch down into Rutland took no time at all. A couple of former thru hikers from Switzerland picked us up, they had met each other hiking the Continental Divide Trail and were in Vermont to show their children what long distance hiking was all about.

"It's funny, back home people ask us what America is like." The husband is telling us, "Only I don't know."

"Hiking is not America. Out here it is something else." The wife adds while bouncing one of her children on her lap to make room for us in the back.

They drop us downtown where we part ways, library, resupply and cheeseburgers all have varying degrees of importance for each of us.

After resupply, blog updates and a few thousand calories of meat and cheese I decide that maybe I want to pack out something from the liquor store. By the time Freyr and I had hiked into Stony Brook Shelter I was sure that drinking and hiking was the right thing to do.

Or at least drinking and staying at the shelter.

Freyr pushed on leaving me behind to drink and think. The drunk hit fast and felt like both an old friend and enemy at the same time. Only something was different. It was almost as if the alcohol in my system was a separate entity. Draped over my shoulders and head like a heavy cloak. Just under my skin, worn against my bare muscle tissue, dulling my mind.

It was the realization that I didn't want it to take over that caused me to start hiking.

My legs knew what to do even if my mind didn't. They found the path, propelled me forward and kept me going. Over steep rock climbs and down an aluminum ladder bolted to a cliff face, past Lakota Lake Lookout. All of it a blur.

This time, sweating, I experienced the alcohol as a completely separate being. Something powerful and ancient, and yet not all powerful.

By the time I stumbled into Wintturi Shelter I had burned most of it out of my system.

I pass my first real SOBO before leaving Vermont.

He's done hiking. Hates it.

"I could be drinking a cold beer and playing pool," he says.

Can't argue with that.

"Thought I'd start liking it a little more but that's not happening."

"Well it took me a long time to start to get into it too, not sure if I'm really there yet, but you have some great trail ahead of you. Not as tough as the New Hampshire and Maine," I say trying to convince him to stick with it a little longer.

At this point he hasn't even done 500 miles.

"Too hot," he says, "I'm soaked and have been all day, water dripping off my face and nose."

I can see it in his eyes, he is done, he wants to go back home, to his bar, to his buddies.

"Well, good luck," I say and continue north. What kept me on the trail? I hated it at least as much as that guy, why did I keep hiking?

And then I pass what looks like a day hiker. Only he is a former thru hiker out for an anniversary day hike to relive it.

"40th anniversary," He says. "Hiked the trail in 1971, was the 35th thru hiker."

"Really? What was your trail name?"

"We didn't have trail names back then. Maybe a couple people did but it didn't really catch on until later."

The look in his eye is so much different from the look in the SOBO's eyes that I can't help but wonder why I met them both in the same day. You can tell that not only did he love his hiking experience, but that he thought about it often.

Didn't I wonder how I would feel about the trail forty years from now just last week?

Weird.

Meanwhile Freyr has decided that he wants to do some night hiking and hands me a 5 Hour Energy at the general store in West Hartford. Happy Hill Shelter was only another 4 miles away and I wanted to call it a day, except I hadn't night hiked before...

And night hiking is an experience.

The whole world around you is black, the trees that shade you during the day block out all light from the moon and stars at night. You can see only right in front of you, and everything else seems infinitely more quiet.

More spooky.

By the time we reach the road Freyr has chafing, it's his first time and he wants to die. Walking like a sweaty cowboy new to riding horseback we cross the state line and walk into Hanover, also known as Hangover, well after midnight looking for the 24 hour pharmacy and some anti-itch cream.

There is no real plan to our hike, we were just walking to walk. And now in Hanover we have no idea where we are going to stay. We head north, out of town, following the AT in hopes of finding a rumored soccer field where you can sleep.

At the stadium we give up. Freyr can't do much walking and we aren't really sure where we are going.

"That could be the soccer field," Freyr says gesturing towards the high school.

"Could be," I say, not really believing it. Then he tries to turn on his headlamp to get a better look.

"Shut that off!" I yell as quietly but forcefully as possible. "Don't give away our position."

He looks at me like I'm crazy and says something about Homeland Security under his breath.

We walk around to some storage sheds in a shadowed corner of the field.

"We can sleep here. Who would come here in the middle of the night?" I ask.

"We did." Freyr says before unrolling his Tyvek ground sheet and inflating his air mattress.

"It's official," Freyr says, "we're hobo's."

I use my pack as a pillow and wonder about skunks.

"What happened to my life? Sleeping behind a school in America?" Freyr is muttering.

The rumor was that Panarchy was the place to stay in Hanover.

It was like an unofficial frat house, empty beer cans and pizza boxes everywhere, clothes piled in heaps for anyone to use, futons rolled up in corners. A giggling, confused girl tries to give us a tour but keeps rolling her eyes trying to figure out what to say. It's 3pm but she looks like she just got out of bed.

"You can't really shock or offend anyone here so do your own thing," she says rocking back and forth on her feet. Drinking and getting high is the norm.

The drinking and hiking experience from the other day weighs heavily on my mind. While Freyr and Neon Mud, who slept in the real soccer field outside of town the same night we arrived, fall in love with the place I am thinking that there is no way I'm drinking in front of a crowd of strangers.

It's a Saturday night and everyone will be drunk or high.

There will be no sleep and everyone will pressure me to drink.

And I will, if I stay here.

When I bump into Freyr and Neon Mud later they are bummed. Panarchy's landlord came in and told them if they were hikers they couldn't stay.

"Our clothes are still in the washing machine." They tell me.

"I wouldn't sweat it too much. No ones around, get a beer, drink. Even if the landlord comes back at some point tonight you guys were invited to stay as guests."

"Just keep a low profile." I add before hiking out of town by myself.

The sweat is pouring off of me when I finally stop to rest, only partially up Mt. Moosilauke.

"So glad I took a shower yesterday."

On a random craving for milk I had walked off the trail to Hikers Welcome Hostel where they immediately placed a free bag of powdered milk in my hands before feeding me some hot dogs another hiker had left behind. That's where Neon Mud and Freyr caught up to me.

They had no problems staying in Hanover, Neon Mud stayed up late drinking with the girls in the basement bar while Freyr attempted to talk to a drunk, rambling girl that was falling asleep on his shoulder. Until her boyfriend showed up to take her away that is.

Now, halfway into the climb up Moosilauke it doesn't seem to want to end.

We stop at cold water spring pouring off the mountain and I try too cool off. Neon Mud just drinks it.

"This is New Hampshire," he says as if he hasn't just been drinking untreated water the whole way. "If you can't drink the water up here the planet is probably dead anyway."

The water is ice cold and we all get goose bumps.

"Mouse tits," Freyr says.

They move on and I keep thinking about lost people. When a person gets lost they will usually tend to navigate downhill, unless they are suicidal, in which case they tend to work towards the highest point on the landscape.

"We must be suicidal."

We climb up over roots and rocks, rain threatens but doesn't show.

Then the blue sky breaks through and we are on one top of the most breathtaking views. It makes you want to break out into song. Luckily the wind was strong enough that no one could hear me.

"The hills are alive with the sound of music."

Though they must have wondered what I was doing twirling around.

By the time I reached Beaver Brook Shelter Neon Mud and Freyr were no where to be found. They had gone on ahead and I'd just assumed they'd be in the shelter already.

"You guys are so out of the Nero the North Club," I say packing my stuff into the shelter with a bunch of SOBO's.

Then the storm that had been threatening all day finally broke. It was amazing in it's power and the volume of water it managed to drop in a short amount of time. That's when Neon Mud and Freyr strolled up and jumped into the shelter.

"How do you guys always get stuck in the rain storms?" I laugh.

"Halfway down the mountain on the wrong trail..."

The SOBO's all look pissed, there is no room for any more hikers, and they are soaking wet.

"Fuck the SOBO's, they're going the wrong way." Freyr adds diplomatically.

In the dream I am riding on top of a powerful truck through snowy, unplowed streets.

I'm on the hood and no one is driving.

It seems natural, if a little out of control.

I can alter the speed and direction of the truck by reaching my right hand down and applying pressure to the deep tread of the moving tire with my fingers.

When a car tries to back out into the road from a driveway on the right I slow the truck down so there isn't a collision. Two things occur to me at the same time, the guy is on his way to work and it is me who is driving that car.

Suddenly being on the hood of the truck seems dangerous instead of driving inside where the brakes are. I hop down and run along the drivers side of the truck, worried that the truck will speed away and open the door. Only I opened the rear door which does me no good.

Drivers door open I jump in to take control of the truck, only now the pedals are morphing and changing shape. I can't seem to focus on them and the truck seems to be picking up speed. I apply the brakes and the truck spins out of control through an icy parking lot coming to rest just inches from a car dealership filled with brand new trucks.

The Whites

In Lincoln the waitress was beautiful.

Her dark black hair tied back behind her head in a pony tail, thick black glasses and wide inviting smile. She had recently moved here from Macedonia and was an avid reader.

"Russian novels in their original Russian," she says in her thick accent. Though she was finding it hard to find the time to read more than a few books a month.

I wasn't sure how to talk to her, my shoulders felt strange and I couldn't figure out what to do with my hands.

"When did I start slouching?" my brain asks me, prodding me to straighten up.

She gets off at 3pm.

And then I stay. We chat outside a coffee shop and hit it off. Finishing the trail is forgotten, I stay in Woodstock renting a room and pick up a part time job. Pretty soon we are living together, marriage is the obvious choice for her citizenship.

After that we vacation in Greece and abroad. My writing improves and I'm happy, really happy.

The Appalachian Trail thru hike was never finished, and there are no regrets.

Then I'm back in the restaurant, staring at my book, unread, in my hands. It all seemed so real and vivid. Like a whole other life played out for me, there if I wanted to take it.

I think of the Dream of the Yellow Millet, one of the stories from China's Eight Immortals.

Lü Yan had fallen asleep cooking yellow millet and saw himself passing his exam and getting a good job. After that it was promotion after promotion and marriage into a wealthy household until finally he was elected Prime Minister.

But with his success and luck came jealousy. The people around him accused him of crimes, his wife betrayed him and his children were killed by bandits. He was left penniless to die in the streets. As he was dying he woke up again, the yellow millet cooking on the stove.

Eighteen years had passed in the dream but only a few minutes had passed while his yellow millet had cooked. In the same way I felt as if four or five years had passed, living happily with this girl I just met.

She comes back to my table and sits down to chat.

"How long have you been out?"

"Four Months," I say finishing off the pancakes.

"Oh, I was expecting you to say three or four days," she says and the conversation flows. She reminds me that she'll be off at 3pm and if I can't make it she will be working tomorrow morning as well.

Out on the sidewalk I'm suddenly not in a hurry to leave town. I lay down in the grass in Cascades Park trying to read, only the words don't make any sense. I quit pretending and put the book away, imagining a whole new unexpected life while families ride inner tubes down the rapids.

Happiness.

Is that what I really want? To be happy?

In Lincoln I have cell service for the first time and call Chet's Place.

He answers on the second ring and asks questions to make sure I'm a thru hiker.

"Where did you start?"

"Where are you going to finish?"

"Which Mountain did you just come off?

When I answer correctly he gives me directions to the One Step at a Time Hostel he runs out of his converted garage. At Chet's the hiker box is said to always be stocked. This rumor brings in the hobo hikers who bum rush the hike box, sampling products and replacing them. A squirt of hand sanitizer here, a dab of shampoo, a single shoe lace taken from a pair of sneakers.

Items are pulled from the box and the hobos who have been out for far too long move them around in some sort of magic pantomime, sensing or subtly detecting the benefits and uses of each item. A secret knowing, like knocking on cantaloupe or reading braille.

With an item or two they shuffle out the front garage door never to be seen again.

I pick a bunk, fully intending on staying to see what would happen with the waitress.

The text message says, URGENT! Call home ASAP.

Calling home does no good as the call is terminated as soon as it is picked up. When I try to call again it is obvious that they have run out of minutes on their cell phone and this immediately puts me in a bad mood.

They call back from my moms ex boyfriend's phone while I'm trying to eat breakfast in McDonald's. They can't hear anything I'm saying, I have to yell into the phone for them to understand and leave my half eaten breakfast to get cold while I step outside to hear about their new big problem.

They have to move, now, out of their apartment and into a new one. And immediately I know that all of the things I stored with them will be gone forever. There is no stability there, never has been. I want to crush the phone in my hands, scream at them, put my fist through the plate glass window.

I don't want to go back to that.

She tells me it's urgent that my work knows if I'm coming back or they are going to fill my position. Outdated information since I had to talk to work when my sister failed to show up.

"I appreciate that you are trying to help but you aren't," I say trying not to raise my voice, "Good luck with the move, I have to go."

I hang up because these calls make me physically sick. I had planned on getting some writing done before heading back to the trail to do the section over Kinsman Mountain and staying at Chet's Place one more night.

Now I want nothing more than to get drunk.

And for the first time since I was in the agony of Lyme's Disease the thought of ending the hike came to mind. In the back of my mind I know that I'll feel different in a few days, and honestly, I didn't want to go back to Rhode Island, not ever.

All of a sudden everyone in town is either fat or old. Families scurry about with fat little whining children and I wish the whole world would burn. A rolling flame from the horizon consumes the mountain, turning trees to ash, people and minivans melt and are gone.

Note to self: Do not accept calls from home.

The first bottle of vodka wasn't big enough and for some reason I thought it would be a good idea to pick up another, bigger bottle before the liquor store closed.

I didn't want to be drunk at Chet's. It seemed disrespectful. And yet there I was, wasted. I stumbled in pretty late and passed out in my bunk. Ashamed.

I wanted to sleep in, sleep off some of the hangover but Chet was there rolling around the garage, seeing who was leaving, who was slack packing. Another thru hiker was giving a few people a ride back to the trail and I hate hitchhiking so I forced myself up. It's a given at this point that I am going to skip the 16 miles over Kinsman Mountain and keep going north from here.

16 miles missed because of a phone call.

Anger, shame.

At the trail head I wasn't completely hungover, just dehydrated. Though my pack felt infinitely heavier.

My new life with the waitress forgotten from the need to keep hiking.

Maybe I don't deserve to be happy.

"They always take thru hikers," Neon Mud was saying.

At least that was the theory about Greenleaf Hut.

Sitting on Mount Lincoln we had only done about six miles for the day.

"Are you in the Nero the North Club or what?" Neon Mud was asking.

The hut system in the Whites was a little different than the shelter system we had been used to so far. The huts were for paying guests, thru hikers could offer to do work for stay in exchange for sleeping on the floor in some out of the way spot, usually the dining room. However, most huts only accepted a couple of hikers at a time, and we were mixing not only with NOBO thru hikers but had started seeing some SOBO's as well.

Greenleaf Hut is over a mile downhill from the trail, hence most hikers don't make the hike down just in case they can't do work for stay. But being so far off the trail and having a hell of a climb out meant that very few people went down there.

"Fuck it, let's do it," I said. The walk across Franconia Ridge had left me awestruck, there was no way I was going to hurry through the Whites.

The huts are all unique and have their own personalities based on location and the current crew or croo, working them. That being said there are a lot of similarities between the huts, at least from a thru hikers perspective.

First you have to approach the head croo member for the day and ask about work for stay. Usually they are friendly but most times you can sense a sort of attitude, like, "I've got too much to do to give your lazy ass free food and a place to sleep."

Which is an accurate and fair assessment on their part. They have to feed and entertain anywhere from 40 to 90 people at a time.

Then if you can do work for stay, and depending on the weather, you will basically sit around and wait, preferably outside so you aren't in the way. Doesn't matter if it's raining and you're cold, you are not a paying customer. While you listen to everyone being served and eating inside you will lounge outside, trying not to seem like the hungry beggar that you are.

The three of us joked that we were outside, "Looking poor to get more."

Holding our empty cups with a sad look like we were about to break into tears. Hopefully guilting paying customers to not eat as much, to make sure there were leftovers.

This is also when everyone speculates on the meal, or more accurately, what the leftovers of the meal will be. Depending on how much was made and how much was consumed will determine how much is left for the hiker trash, I mean thru hikers. But it is usually amazing food. A soup, sometimes with homemade bread, mashed potatoes, chicken and rice, stuffed shells.

And you have to remember that for each of these huts the majority of this food was packed in on the backs of croo members.

But you still have to wait while the croo cleans up and the members play card games and chat. No matter when you finally walk inside they will tell you that it will be a few more minutes.

And while you wait everyone wants to talk to you, and ask the same questions you have been getting repeatedly the entire hike.

"How long have you been hiking?"

"How did you get the time off of work?"

"How many miles a day do you do?'

The one I hate the most is, "What you are doing is terrific. I wish I could do that."

I simply do not believe you. Most of the people that said that to me were romanticizing the hike, to "wish" means you have no intention of doing it but are trying to be polite. So thanks, but it comes off as condescending most of the time.

Then it's lights out.

Move the tables and benches around in the dining area and find a place to sleep on the floor.

Then in the morning you have to be up early and get out so the croo can serve breakfast. If you did your work for stay the night before you can leave before breakfast, or you can stick around for some cold pancakes with no butter and cold syrup. You may even be able to score a spoonful of scrambled eggs or a piece of bacon if the stars line up just right.

It's in the Whites where we start arguing about the exact definition of a thru hiker.

It started in Zealand Falls Hut and the argument followed us down the trail. There was an older guy staying there, a paid guest, who came outside to sit with us, after he had finished his breakfast and we waited for ours.

"Good to meet some fellow thru hikers," he said lighting up his post meal cigarette.

"You're a thru hiker?" Neon Mud asks incredulous.

"Yep, tenth year," he says stretching out his legs.

"Tenth year thru hiking?"

"One more section to go after this and I'll be done."

I can see the look in Neon Mud's eyes, he wants to kill this guy.

"That's not a thru hike."

"Sure it is, a thru hike is a designation for anyone who walks the length of the trail from end to end," the guy says misquoting the ATC guidelines.

Neon Mud rages while we hike.

"The problem is that the thru hiker rate of completion is increasing. They're too lax in what they call a thru hiker."

"No section hikers!"

"Fuck section hikers."

"How about no more than three sections?"

"Maybe four 500 mile sections but that's it."

"No flip flopping?"

"Isn't that almost the same as taking a few zero's?"

"What? How?"

You get off trail for a couple of days and come right back to it, you just happen to be at the other end."

"I don't know, it feels like it should be considered cheating."

"But is it?"

"A thru hike is doing it all at once. Anything less is just a hike."

It's raining and the mud and rocks slow us down, still we cover the 5 miles to Ethen Pond Shelter in under an hour. The conversation driving us into a speed hike.

New Boots shows up. We call him that because he has the same pair of boots as Neon Mud, only his are in much better condition.

"My mama told me not to step in mud puddles," he says showing off his crisp looking boots. "Did 700 miles in these."

Meanwhile Neon Mud had done over 1,800 miles in them on this hike alone.

He was staying to have lunch and avoid the rain, so we kept moving. Probably wondering why other thru hikers weren't as friendly as he was.

"Fucking section hikers."

The joke about the Whites is that they are called that because that's the view you get, white.

In fact it looked exactly like my view from Clingman's Dome. And Grayson Highlands.

And Roan Mountain.

After Webster Mountain we thought the climbing was done.

Not by a long shot.

Some of it is daunting straight up, hand over hand climbing. Most of it is wet rocks covered in bright green lichens that are slippery as snot. Meanwhile you are cold and wet and there is zero visibility. Neon Mud was falling at least a couple of times every mile, our hands are numb and wrinkled and if we stop hiking the cold creeps into your bones.

We were having so much fun.

I fall for the first time that day and Freyr points and laughs, then manages to slip and fall on exactly the same rock giving me a chance to return the favor.

You climb up, you climb down.

On the steep downward climbs we stop to watch Neon Mud, not so much for his safety but for our own entertainment.

Then we pass a 60 year old lady on the trail all by herself.

"Don't worry dear, my husband went on ahead to the hut," she says as if that would make me feel better. The climbs are pretty treacherous and the fact that her husband left her out here alone gets me a little angry.

The three of us slow down and watch her make a steep descent then hike a little farther down the trail for a break. She takes forever to show up and just when we are about to go back for her she rounds the trail.

"Did you boys wait for me?"

"Just wanted to make sure you made it through the worst of it."

The wind whips heavy rain across the open areas threatening to push us off the boardwalks and into the fragile vegetation. When we catch up to three hikers carrying a single day pack amongst them I know we are close.

Mizpah Hut.

When we get inside the place is packed. But we hadn't seen any other thru hikers so we figured we were in like Flynn.

"Sorry, there are two thru hikers ahead of you," the croo member says.

"What? Who?" we ask looking around.

"But I can probably take you if you don't mind doing work in the morning." What else are we going to do? Besides the storm is only supposed to get worse outside, which is probably why she agreed to let us stay on.

The problem is that there are no other thru hikers in the hut.

When the older lady we passed comes in she is told to put her pack in with ours, she is doing work for stay.

"There must be some kind of mistake, didn't you say you hiked in from Crawford Notch?"

"Yes, it was my husbands idea."

Her husband, the guy that had left her out there by herself, had hiked into the hut to get a work for stay position for the both of them even though their "thru hike" consisted of the 6 miles up from their car. It was his bright idea to save them some money.

When they announced that a few AT thru hikers would be staying for the night he gladly waved to the crowd eating in the dining room below.

I almost grabbed his ankles and threw him over the railing.

Pretty sure Freyr and Neon Mud would have looked the other way.

"Fucking section hikers."

"Not even a section hiker!"

We knew we were close to Lake of the Clouds Hut when we heard the sound of the wind generator long before the lodge loomed dark through the clouds.

Overnight the storm had worsened. It was cold and raining and it seemed as if the entire world had been plunged inside a cloud. Even the thought of missing the views for the entire presidential range didn't stop us from enjoying a truly unique hiking experience.

Despite having hiked less than 5 miles we decided to take a chance and ride out the storm in hopes of having a clear day on the summit of Mt. Washington.

Lake of the Clouds Hut is truly an experience to have before you die. In the morning I woke up to a sunrise outside the dining room window that was breathtaking. The clouds had filled in the valley and the sun had turned everything shades of pink and purple. The view seemed to go on forever and I still couldn't get enough of it.

"The worst part about hiking is that I wake up happy every day. So happy that I feel guilty when I talk to people back home and they tell me their problems," the hiker next to me says between sips of coffee.

"If I could give everyone back home a gift it would be this," I said.

Even though the storm had passed the wind gusts were still up to 50 miles per hour and the wind chill was below freezing. That didn't stop the rainbow colored assortment of hikers from making the rocky climb up Mt. Washington.

Halfway to the top from lake of the Clouds I stopped and sat down on a rock. Not because I was tired or that the climb was too strenuous. I stopped because the moment was so perfect. The clouds were white and glowing, the hut was below me on one side, on the other was a plume of black smoke from the cog railway making it's run to the top.

"Everything is glorious," another thru hiker says in passing.

It really is.

The cold wind blows through me and I'm not even sure I took a breath in the 20 minutes that I sat there.

Last Push

Wildcat Mountain is allegedly one of the toughest climbs on the AT.

I wouldn't know.

You see, long before I started hiking my research had included a list of things people had wished they had done different on their thru hike. I figured this was going to be a once in a lifetime hike and I wanted to do it right.

Besides the usual "swim more", "spend less time in town" stuff one of the things people had said was to take the chair lift up Wildcat Mountain.

I never thought it would happen, I wanted to hike past every white blaze, and yet the notation was added in the margin of my thru hikers' companion. And far from being tired or frustrated I still found myself riding a gondola to the top.

No excuses.

And I didn't feel guilty about it one bit.

Something had changed about me in the Whites. I couldn't quite put my finger on it. There was a sense of calm that hadn't been there before. Despite being in no hurry I was hiking faster than the lazy days of Nero the North.

When I stopped for lunch there were a couple of weekend hikers at the shelter, a father and his son making dinner. While they had hiked over two days to get here I had done the same amount of miles in only a handful of hours. They planned on staying, I was planning on hiking ahead.

"I've had a lot of practice," is all I could say when they marveled at the ground covered.

They had been trying to set up their stove before I arrived and after I had started eating they had managed to warm up a

Mountain House meal in a pot. Which they then proceeded to spill onto the shelter floor.

"A thru hiker would still eat it," I said knowing that they would never.

They laughed politely trying to judge if I was joking or serious and then broke out a couple more meals. They had easily eight days worth of food for the hike from Pinkham Notch to US 2 in Gorham, NH. Twenty miles, two nights for them, one day for me.

And they had taken the gondola too.

That's when I noticed it again, I was different. I wasn't pissed off at the loss of food, didn't get mad that they had all expensive brand name gear, wasn't even bothered by the fact that they didn't seem to know what they were doing.

After offering them a few tips I wished them luck and was on my way.

The first time I really appreciated the difference between the SOBO and NOBO experience was at the Maine/New Hampshire border. It wasn't so much the hard descent over large boulders that I floated down and a SOBO would have to climb. It was the fact that there was a sign welcoming you to Maine but not one welcoming you to New Hampshire.

Just outside of Bly Gap was the Georgia/North Carolina sign marking your crossing into another state. It had been a reason to celebrate, an accomplishment. It seems that there is no similar sign for SOBO's.

Their journey is something completely different from what I experienced.

It was the rocky descent which caused the most problems for other hikers. Even thru hikers were taking their time, some were even removing their backpacks for stability. They would stagger into Carlo Col Shelter, having planned on going farther for the night, only to have the incoming thunder and lightning storm change their plans.

A couple of college kids come in dragging their packs. The rest of their group is stuck back on the rocks, refusing to climb down. They unpack ropes and flashlights and go back to see if they can bring them down before the storm moves in. A couple stay behind because one of them has to go to the bathroom, only they didn't pack out toilet paper.

She is gathering up handfuls of leaves when I offer my toilet paper.

The rain starts in a little harder as the college students straggle in like they were returning from war. They look at us in the shelter, dry and all smiles, while they have to set up their tents in the drizzle.

For some reason I think of my father, "Hardship breeds character."

Maine has a couple of highlights everyone needs to experience.

First is Goose Eye Mountain, if it isn't windy don't go. Though it is hard not to imagine it anything but storm like gusts of wind. Eyes watered and the straps from my pack became dangerous, whipping around in the wind, plastic clips slamming into my hands like hammers.

The wind is so strong that I could lean into it and still be held upright. I would jump into it and spread my arms and let it carry me a couple feet backwards. Then to climb down one side and back up the other peak felt like I was in a giant playground.

Then of course there is the Mahoosuc Notch.

Said to be either the toughest or the most enjoyable mile of the Appalachian Trail I can tell you from my experience that it by far the most fun.

Luckily it was drizzling by the time we got there after having run down the south peak of Fulling Mill Mountain. And I mean ran. I was jacked up on adrenaline and ready to take on the Notch. When I saw it uncontrollable laughter took over my body and I ran at it, bounding up and over and under boulders.

I pass another freshman orientation group who seem to be standing still on the trail, ever so cautious. I want to roar at them as I run by only I didn't want any of them slipping. Full rain gear and pack covers they were shivering and nervous. By the time their guide told them to step aside to let me pass I was already gone.

Soaking wet in a t-shirt and shorts.

Grinning like an idiot.

Then up the Mahoosuc Arm. Deceivingly simple at first before it goes straight up a waterfall. And then there are no blazes, I'm climbing with an intense instinct of where the trail should be, too jacked up not to be confident.

It could be the trail, it could be just runoff.

Then at the top the first faded white blaze worn away but still faintly visible on a rock.

"White Blaze!" I yell out loud, listening to my voice echo down into the canyon.

The climb has me pumped.

I run down and around Speck Pond to the shelter, so dehydrated I want to lick plants as I run by, so dehydrated and out of my mind I don't bother filtering the water from a stream for making Gatorade.

It was only slightly off color.

Pretty sure Gatorade kills Giardia.

Then I have the dream again.

It's night time and I'm roaming around a city with a large knife in each hand.

There is no mood or emotion attached to the whole situation, I'm just hurrying around, looking at everything and very conscious of the fact that I shouldn't be carrying the knives so openly. When people are around I try to hide them behind my arms.

Try to be inconspicuous.

Then I'll pass a knife on the ground and have to grab it. I am compelled to pick it up and carry that too. Soon I am carrying a large selection of knives bundled in my arms.

Which makes it awkward to go into public places and board the city bus.

When I try to pay bus fare some of the knives fall from my arms and clatter to the floor.

That's when I wake up.

Hurricane Irene?

Yes please.

Everyone seems worried about their hike, I am considering the possibility of riding out the hurricane in the woods, on the trail. Keep hiking through the worst of it and have the time of my life.

Except instead I end up splitting a room with Freyr and Aces at the White Wolf Inn.

And we zero through the storm watching bad cable TV and staring off into space.

When Freyr and I try to hitchhike out of town after the storm has blown through there are no cars. It seems the bridge out of town heading back towards the AT had been washed out. By the time we get back to the trail my knees hurt so much I'm not sure if I can make the climb. All my momentum seems gone.

Now Maine just seems like a bunch or rocks and roots and mud.

I hate Maine.

I want to be finished with the trail.

"If Maine had been anywhere else on the trail," another thru hiker was saying to me, "maybe I would have enjoyed it."

When he throws his pack down in the shelter he notices a missing the plastic clip for the chest strap. He becomes exasperated searching for it and eventually comes up with it in his hand.

"If I hadn't been able to put it back together I would have quit right there," he says without a trace of humor in his voice.

Everyone is worn down. Forget Nero the North, I just want to go home.

Not that I have a home I remind myself. I just don't want to be here, to have to do miles everyday. To have to ford rivers and slip in the mud and hop from rock to rock on what is supposed to be the trail.

Hitchhiking out of Monson reminds me of just how much I hate hitchhiking.

People with empty cars that won't make eye contact.

Guys in pickup trucks can't stop to let you hop in the back.

People are at their lowest and I have to force a smile, laugh it off and try not to yell or freak out like some other hikers do.

Then a pickup truck pulls over and the guy clears random junk from the passenger seat. There is always stuff on the seat and floor that they assure you is okay to move out of the way or step on.

Not even 15 minutes on the side of the road to get a ride out of town and I'm fuming, complaining about the downfall of mankind.

Nobody cares.

Shouldn't hiking have mellowed me out a little more than this? Wasn't I little more mellow just a couple hundred miles ago?

And he takes me right to the trail.

There is some boring small talk, usually that's the most you can hope for. The worst is when they are boring *and* won't shut up. You want to ask them to pull over to let you out.

"Thanks, I'll keep trying."

But you stick with the ride and wave and smile as they drive away leaving you exactly where you'd hoped to be, and in five minutes you forget everything about them.

God, I'm so shallow.

It's important to me to get here, back to the trail, but my brain isn't thinking about why they would help a perfect stranger get down the road. My brain is thinking about being done.

I laugh to myself when I read the caution sign at the edge of the 100 Mile Wilderness. It warns every hiker that you should have a minimum 10 days worth of supplies.

100 miles is like five days hiking and I have maybe six days worth of food.

10 days is just being silly.

The last little bit of the sign nags at me where it says the difficulty of this section should not be underestimated.

Go fuck yourself.

But what the hell, I'm already here. It's not like I'm going to hitchhike back into town, resupply, then come back.

You cross this log bridge that looks like someone pushed a ladder across a stream and suddenly your in it, the 100 Mile Wilderness everyone has been talking about since the Whites.

And for the first time I am in love with Maine.

Somehow it feels like now I'm really in Maine. Everything is new and different.

Like an adventure within the adventure.

The ultimate end, the final lap on this racecourse called the AT.

I didn't know there was going to be a road in the middle of the Hundred Mile Wilderness

I was hiking fast, soaked from the light rain, running ahead of the thunder and lightning that I knew was approaching, but when I saw it I stopped dead in my tracks.

Not the road but the cooler bag on the side trail. Trail Magic in the middle of the Hundred Mile Wilderness? I knew I should be moving but it was so worth getting soaked to be able to drink a cold soda.

Then there were cars lined up on this dirt road I hadn't expected. People and families heading back to their cars. I hadn't realized that the Gulf Hagas was such a tourist destination.

Lightning flashed and the thunder rolled in with more rain.

Coat-less families in tank tops with empty water bottles and digital cameras they were trying to shield from the rain. Large groups of people fleeing across the west branch of the Pleasant River were in a panic. They didn't want to get stuck out here.

"You're going the wrong way." More than one tourist pointed out.

The farther up the trail I got the more the crowd thinned, the harder the rain fell and the louder the thunder became.

"Aren't you worried about the river crossing?!" a couple stopped me on the trail to ask.

"There's another river crossing?" I wondered, trying to remember what the guidebook had said.

"No, I mean going back," the husband had to yell over the sound of the torrential rain.

"I'm not going back." I smiled. His strange, questioning look was making it hard to force back the laughter. He looked down at the ground as if trying to process what I said, looked back up at me and scratched behind his ear.

I turned and hiked on thinking just how ominous that sounded.

A wicked smile crossed my face and I thought of him telling people about how I knew I was going to die if I was found dead.

Lightning flashes again, closer and the thunder rolls through my bones. I smile for the solitude the threatening storm has provided, happy and at peace, soaking wet.

Not a care in the world.

Then one more couple bounces by, leather hat, raw wood walking stick, she's wearing the pack, he has dreadlocks. Hippies I think to myself, they're smiling too, but in a happy way.

My smile isn't happy?

Then I'm alone, really alone.

I slip and fall in the mud twisting my fingers just in time to prevent them from bending backwards and taking the full weight of my body and pack.

"You might need those," my brain says.

I lay there on the ground, a little over a mile from the river crossing. Over a mile since I've seen anyone else. Every slippery rock is the end of me.

The lightning flash and crack of thunder happens simultaneously.

The storm is all around me. A little more than 100 feet away the lightning hits the ground, and the crack isn't so much a noise as it is a feeling your heart reacts to. Every flash causes me to jump instantaneously away from the nearest tree, hoping to be quick enough that I'm not in contact with the ground or close enough for the electricity to arc over.

I realize that I am going to die.

Not in an abstract way, but also not necessarily right now. It is simply a realization that at some point I will not exist.

"Killed by lightning so close to the end?" I say looking up at the angry, dark sky.

"Come on, that's too cliché, even for you."

Except that my death is inevitable. Every slippery rock from a stream crossing cries out for my skull, ominous broken branches sharpened, poised ready to sink into my soft flesh when I fall upon them, slipping in the mud.

A crack the lightning hits again, this time it sizzles close by.

So many ways to die.

Fall into the stream unable to move as brown wet cold water kills me through hypothermia.

Crack.

And of course to be killed by lightning.

I had imagined death before, but not like this.

The world would not disappear if I was dead. It would go on as it had before, just as it always has. I would not come back as a ghost, I would not be haunting any place, leaving your toilet seat up or letting your cats out of your apartment.

To die like this out here doesn't scare me, it just makes me sad that I wasted so much time drinking away large chunks of my life. In a way I was dead already, before, sitting there in my apartment back home going through the motions, day-to-day, month-to-month. Paying bills but not doing much else.

If I die now at least things make sense. I see where I went wrong. What I was doing.

Punishing myself.

I didn't deserve to live and so I lived as if I was already dead.

Death, dying out here seemed both perfect and fitting.

I'd like to tell you that I thought, "I want to live!" or some other cliche. You know, something palatable for human consumption. But that wasn't the thought that occurred to me.

"You want to kill me, I'm right here!" I yelled up into the sky.

The tall trees stood on either side of the path around me and I stopped and waited, surprised by just how dark it had become. Had I been so wrapped up in fighting myself that I hadn't noticed how late it had become?

Listening to the rain, feeling it's cold embrace, there was a flash of light so intense, so close by that I felt as if I were inside it, and yet I didn't flinch. A second later the sharp crack echoes down through the trees like a gunshot.

The storm was moving away.

I smiled in the dark wet afternoon and started hiking again.

I was alive.

Summiting

After five days in the 100 Mile Wilderness entering Baxter State Park felt like I was being ushered into a palace. The arch of color around me, greens, reds and yellows of the leaves starting to change. The trail itself was pine needles, soft and welcoming.

The threshold to the end.

Then you check in at Baxter Stream Campground, I was Hiker #276, and sleep in the Birches where the limit is one night. One night with a sandwich and soda from Abol Bridge felt I was king of the world.

The next morning you get up early to summit, stop at Thoreau Spring for water to lunch at the top, at the sign.

Top of Katahdin, top of the world.

I did this, I persevered.

There is no stream of energy or some sudden realization that hits you at the peak. In fact it is a mixture of emotions that is hard to talk about. Sadness that you are done, happiness that you have finished.

Satisfaction.

People can be sports stars or movie stars but this is what I did. I walked over 2,000 miles for five months without quitting, without giving up, hiking through the rain, through the pain.

It's more than just taking my picture next to the sign.

Luckily I have a clear day to summit and I have the peak all to myself for almost an hour.

I am so content allowing the wind to blow through me, to lay on the rocks in the sun.

Perfect.

All I want now is a gallon of milk, a pair of jeans and a haircut.

Let's get the hell off this mountain.

Appendix

Stats

Hike Time – 153 Days

Zero's – 22

Original Budget - $2,500

$ Spent - $3,687

> Basically "On Trail" costs.

> Gear purchased while on the trail is included while the gear purchased before the hike is not.

> Overage in my budget is roughly equal to the cost of gear purchased in Damascus and the I-81 Interchange at Troutville, as well as the doctors visit for Lyme Disease in Pittsfield, MA.

Average Cost Per Day - $24.10

> If I hadn't upgraded gear on the trail - $16.33/day

Average Cost Per Mile - $1.70

Miles

> 14 miles a day average overall

> 16.65   miles a day average taking zero days into account

> 16.66

Biggest Mile Days – 32.2 to Double Springs Shelter from Kincora Hostel

31.4 to Gran Anderson Shelter from Church of the Mountain Hostel in DWG

Shortest Mile Day - .9 miles, from George Outerbridge Shelter to Palmerton, PA (Though I did then walk the 2 miles into town)

1.6 miles from Upper Goose Pond Cabin into Lee,MA

Stuff You Don't Need to Pack

Of course what you pack and why is a personal choice, as well as how much weight you are comfortable with. However there were a few things on the trail that I kept seeing over and over again that, well, you might want to consider before attempting a thru hike of your own.

1. Deodorant – Wash yourself once in a while, that's what rivers are for

2. An Umbrella – Originally it was an item that I considered bringing, then I realized that at no point in my hike did I ever utter the phrase, "I wish I had an umbrella."

3. Trowel – It's a shovel for when you poop. Why are you pooping in the woods? Use a privy, or for gods sake do it in town. Plan ahead.

4. Rain Pants – I packed them at the start, used them as a layer on Roan Mountain so I didn't freeze to death while sleeping, but it was stupid, they serve no purpose.

5. A Crank Radio – So you don't need batteries you are going to lug around a hand crank generator just in case you can get a radio signal? Are you kidding?

6. A Giant Knife, Ax, Saw or Machete - Unless you are a scary hobo that purchased all of their gear from Wal-Mart and refuses to "Go Back", then yeah, it's appropriate, and maybe even required.

Regrets

Regrets are few though there were a couple that you may want to consider for your own thru hike. FYI, I did not include the regret that I should have hiked the AT a long time ago.

- Missing the view at Clingman's Dome because it was fogged in
- Too many zero's in Damascus for Trail Days
- The zero at Wood's Hole Hostel
- Skipping Franks for the Memories in Buena Vista because I was low on funds
- Spending too much money on new gear while on the trail
- Not tracing my feet at the beginning of the trip for comparison afterward
- Not having better mosquito protection through New Jersey and New York

Honestly, to that I would like to add that I regret that I cannot be friends in everyday life with the kinds of people that I met on the trail every single day.

But that is not a regret from the hike, it's a result of the hike.

About the Author

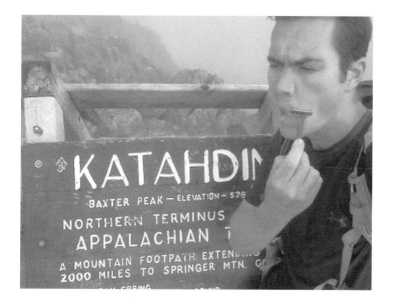

Chris Miller is a writer and traveler who is working towards location independence by making the majority of his income from online ventures.

He thru hiked the Appalachian Trail in 2011 and has ridden a bicycle over 2,500 miles on the East Coast Greenway to help raise money for Meals on Wheels.

After Katahdin
by Chris "Cleanshave" Miller

Imagine living in the woods for five or six months.

No job, no worries.

Now imagine being thrust back into the 'real' world to try and rebuild your life. Forced to get a job and find a place to live.

This is the reality faced by many Appalachian Trail thru hikers upon summiting Mount Katahdin. What do you do when you no longer have to hike everyday?

In 2011 Chris "Cleanshave" Miller had finished his Appalachian Trail thru hike and returned to his hometown. Without an apartment, with very little in the way of savings he quickly found that some of the most difficult hurdles faced by a thru hiker aren't always on the trail.

Sometimes it's readjusting to the world you left behind.

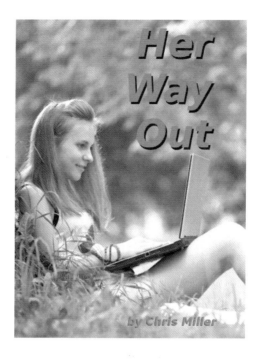

"Suddenly she became aware of her ability to make money online, and as she grew more confident she was able to escape all the little problems that pulled her in too many directions."

That is the sentence that served as the guiding light for the stories that follow, and it is also one that you will be able to confidently say to yourself as you read and apply some of these ideas in your life.

- Have you ever thought about making money online or working from home but found that everyone was trying to "sell" you on their system?

- Have you been swamped by all the options available without knowing which one was for you?

- Have you been unsure about how to get started making money online?

If so these short stories are for you. Each of these five short stories covers a different aspect of how various women started and succeeded in making money online. While each story is fiction they are all based on real life situations that have happened to real women just like you.

ThingsGoingSmoothly.com